ASTRAL WAR

Your Soul is the Battlefield

LENNART SVENSSON

978-0-6456700-1-1

Astral War
Lennart Svensson

Thema Classification: QRYC (Esoteric Traditions), VX (Mind, Body, Spirit).

MANTICORE PRESS
WWW.MANTICORE.PRESS

CONTENTS

INTRODUCTION

Since the dawn of time, light has battled against the dark. This is *the astral war, the psychic war, the magic war.* I briefly discussed this in my previous book (*Actionism – How to Become a Responsible Man*). In it, I used the term "frequency war" for the phenomenon.

The astral war does not involve real weapons. There is no physical clash between armies in this conflict. Nonetheless, this battle is a fierce one.

I intend to delve deeper into the "immaterial war" complex in this book. To be an astral warrior, you need a robust ethical doctrine. Fighters in the astral war need a compelling narrative; they need something to shape them and prepare them for battle – they need "a moral equivalent of war" – and *voilà*, this, the book you are now reading could be seen as that document.

This book is a stand-alone, self-contained work. However, my philosophy of life, called Actionism, provides a background for it, which was revealed in *Actionism – How to Become a Responsible Man* (2017). This contained a summation of Actionist thought titled "Actionism in 36 Words," which included the following formula:

> Actionism is about summoning your Will to lead your Thought, merging the two to Will-Thought and affirming the Inner Light, a spark of the Divine Light. To all this, saying 'I AM' is the performative confirmation.

In other words, Actionism is a philosophy of life with willpower and vision at the fore. It is a mindful attitude to existence, with strains of Western and Eastern traditional thought forming the foundation and which creates a gestalt system, incorporating figures such as Ernst Jünger, Plotinus, Evola, Castaneda, and Rudolf Steiner as popular icons.

Actionism is a traditional self-help creed but isn't solely focused on the individual. History and society's current state also play a role; it all harmonizes in holistic splendor. This holistic, micro- and macrocosm approach is also dominant in this volume.

This book focuses on the topic of the astral war – the general nature of it (chapters 1-4, and again in 15-19) and the mindful weapon you need to fight it (chapters 8-14).

The book begins by explaining the concept of "astral war," for which we have synonyms like *propaganda war, energy war, infra war,* and *spirit war.* Specifically, chapters 1 and 2 illustrate the general nature of the astral war. Chapter 4 revisits an aspect of the Actionist concept, *Action as Being,* now seen as *War as Being.* This serves to provide instructions for the astral warrior.

The following three chapters explore the subjects of holism versus reductionism, God, and the artistic element of esotericism. This portrays my general, *mindful* worldview; these chapters bestow the necessary background for the astral war reality.

In *Actionism,* I briefly mentioned the subject of "mental energy." I elaborate upon this in chapters 8-14, referring to it as "Human Magnetism," *od, ka, vril,* et cetera. This is the energetic ammunition the astral war is fought with.

Finally, in chapters 15-19, I return to the subject of astral war proper, reflecting on it from different perspectives, such as providing literary examples demonstrating the phenomenon.

The zeitgeist of today is materialistic. Therefore, to oppose it, you must be an idealist, an Actionist, or a similar type of perennial missionary. You can only change the materialistic miasma of the current times by being a mindful idealist, a man with the divine spark within who embodies the divine idea.

This idea is realized by saying: I am. And the importance of this uttering was duly explained in *Actionism.*

Once more: I am.

I am a willful operator in the vein of Actionism, pro-actively affirming my own being.

I stand for "initiation, inebriation, inspiration." I stand for mindful, perennial tradition against the forces of reductive materialism ruling the world.

In the materialist miasma that is abundant today, I weaponize my "I AM." I sum up my will-thought and passion for fighting in the perpetual spirit, propaganda, and energy wars, which are all components of the astral war. The astral war is immaterial, a spectral war, a holy war fought on the electronic bastions of the 21st century.

And again: I am.

I am an astral warrior, a spirit warrior, an Actionist – total man, absolute man, acknowledging the whole against reductive nonsense, the big picture against fragmentation. I stand for gods and devas, heroes and heroines, myth and legend, freedom of speech, freedom of expression, and artistic freedom.

I am an astral warrior. I *am* the astral war. I have fought it for as long as I can remember.

And I know: you can't win this war if you don't possess the will to win.

You can't win this war if you lack the vision for victory.

You can't win the astral war if you don't acknowledge your spiritual being.

And that acknowledgment, that affirmation, do I need to spell it out again, is – I AM.

I AM the unstoppable fire.

I AM the Metal Messiah and the Total Teacher, the thunder of the tundra, the pilgrim of the Palearctic zone and beyond.

I *want* to be this preacher and teacher. I *want* to be at this specific moment in history. I affirm my being, my inner light.

I AM the last court of appeal of esoteric ontology.

I AM the last prophet of the I AM. After me, all mindful people will sooner or later have acknowledged their I AM. And then the Age of Aquarius will be realized. A new golden age for man will dawn.

The first prophet of the I AM was Manu. Q.v. *Mānava–dharma–śāstra*.

The second prophet of the I AM was Jesus Christ. Q.v. The Gospel of John.

The third prophet of the I AM was Rudolf Steiner. Q.v. *Das Johannesevangelium* (1910).

The fourth and possibly last prophet of the I AM is me. Q.v. *Actionism*. And after my work is done, the Golden Age will be here, enabling a traditional society where the strong are just, the weak secure, and the peace preserved. All people will then live securely in their place of origin. Each ethnicity will be given its due. The law will be upheld by a judiciary, a police force, and a military free from co-opting by mindless forces. Media will stop brainwashing people and instead strive for the truth. The academia will teach the truth and not be a venue of dualistic regimentation. Hospitals and pharmaceutical ventures will cure people, not poison them. Art will once again focus on eternal values such as truth, will, and faith.

After imperialism is rooted out, the peace restored, and traditional borders secured, man will venture out into space for real.

After rectifying the current chaos harassing Earth, mankind will face a new dawn, a new renaissance, and a virtual Day of Freedom in the sign of Aquarius. The formal epochal break came in the autumn of 2011; mankind reached a new level in its development, according to C.J. Calleman and others. Now, it is left for every individual to realize the shift within.

This, for its part, is "the second coming of Christ."

For Jesus Christ will not incarnate in the flesh again and go through the arduous journey to become a studied youth, a preacher, and a teacher. Others are currently doing that job all over the globe. Teachers sent by the light.

The virtual second coming of Christ is people realizing their I AM impulse within.

Then, and only then, will the Day of Freedom be a reality.

But essentially, it is simple.

If all of you wanted it, the Day of Freedom would dawn right now. The only thing it takes is relaxing – taking a deep breath – being calm, cool, and collected – and saying, I AM.

Härnösand in February 2023

LENNART SVENSSON

1. ASTRAL WAR

Awar is raging on the planet today. It is called the astral war.

This is the primary nomenclature for the conflict. However, it can also be called *spirit war, holy war, propaganda war, media war, info war, frequency war, energy war, psychic war, silent war, infra war, virtual war, spectral war,* or *war of nerves.*, Furthermore, in German, we have the concepts of *Kulturkampf* and *Weltanschauungskrieg.*

Whatever name is used, this battle is an ancient one. It has existed since the dawn of time and the primordial emergence of dark and light. The Demiurge stands for the dark; God stands for the light.

The crux of the Astral War looks beyond the battles fought on material battlefields. We must gaze beyond material war to perceive the energy war, the spirit war, the astral war.

In *Actionism,* I briefly touched upon this phenomenon. "Astral war" proper wasn't mentioned, but its synonym, "frequency war," was. In *Actionism* Part Two – The Macrocosm, I wrote about the frequency war, globalism versus nationalism, secret history, and other similar topics. All of these are, in other words, examples of astral war.

The premise of the astral war is that the zeitgeist no longer favors conventional war. Instead, it favors another type of war – the astral war. We are all fighting the astral war. No one is neutral. Every mind-endowed, thinking, living human being is a spiritual warrior. Surfing on the net and being exposed to its images and texts is astral warfare. Reading books is astral war. Talking to the man in the street is astral war.

In this conflict, you must participate as a mindful operator, not a mindless one. The Demiurge quickly devours the mindless actor. But, on the other hand, the *mindful* actor exudes light and fights his way with a virtual lightsaber.

The astral war is a somewhat abstract war, not a physical, old-school, boots-on-the-ground war. However, even such highly tangible action becomes part of the astral war when given a propagandistic spin. This is the main reason The Powers That Be still fight material wars: to conceptualize them as part of the imperialistic narrative, of their biased view of good vs. evil, the Empire vs. indigenous peoples, for example.

This is all in harmony with the concept of "4g warfare," the modern type of warfare where the propagandistic, immaterial element is given a prominent place. Old-school warfare was fought with invasions, mass armies, and industrial mobilization; today's war is primarily an astral war, a propaganda war directed at our minds.

It is a total war, total in the sense that no act, no thought, no feeling is unimportant. The mindful actor controls his every thought and emotion, thus avoiding being brainwashed. But, on the other hand, the mindless actor has no control over his thoughts and emotions and is virtual cannon fodder in this conflict.

The astral war is a war for your soul. Your soul is the battlefield.

And since "the soul is everything" – *idam sarvam, yad ayam ātmā* – the astral war is also a total war.

No one is neutral in this war. Therefore, the only viable exemption warrant would be a declaration of insanity signed by a psychiatrist.

So, those of you who are clinically insane, step aside, leave the battlefield, and go to the loony bin.

The rest of you must learn how to fight the astral war – and win. You must know how to oppose the Demiurge, *the Eagle* Castaneda speaks of, the blind idiot god Azathoth, writhing at the center of the cosmos to the idiot piping of a demon flute.

We Actionists are opposing this darkness. We are opposing the Demiurge, bent on devouring our souls. Instead, we strive for the light, acknowledging and maintaining the soul light, the Inner Light, a fragment of the Divine Light.

We are the Army of the Light fighting the Army of the Dark. See my novel *Redeeming Lucifer* for a vision of such a battle.

To survive in the astral war, you must live a mindful life.

The following is what living a mindful life is and its counterpart.

To live a life connected to biased media, constantly being offended by events, perpetually yearning for utopia, continually fearing hell – the person living such a life is insane. The Empire controls him. He is merely cannon fodder in the astral war.

On the contrary, a person who has will controlling his thought lives in equanimity. He entertains his mind with reading, deliberation, and meditation. Therefore, that person is viable astral warrior material.

One must control every thought and emotion to prevail in this war. The only alternative is to drift like a ship without a sail on capricious tides controlled by the Demiurge. You choose.

You must support freedom of the will, freedom of expression, freedom of thought, and freedom from oppression by The Powers That Be.

Information is light. To enable the flow of information is to fight for the light. Conversely, to hinder information is to support the dark side.

The astral war needs soldiers – metapolitical actors – *you*. To serve the light calls for action – dedicated action – weaponized mindfulness. Jünger said this in *Heliopolis*: "There's nothing stronger than a dreamer turned to action." To me, this is the astral warrior *in nuce*.

2. YOUR SOUL IS
THE BATTLEFIELD

The astral war takes place in a grey area. It is a total war in which one cannot remain neutral.

This is a war aimed at the victory of the light, a war of the forces of life against the forces of death. However, until this victory is secured, a sinister everyday factor awaits the proactive fighter, existence in a virtual no man's land, a spectral land. It is a *psychological landscape.* However, it is an environment you can influence with willpower and thought.

"The victory of the light" is the goal. But in this struggle, you must get used to the everyday reality of a loveless, rather unthankful struggle.

So, I welcome you to the combat zone of the astral war, the magic war, the spirit war, the energy war...

This is a virtual area of mindful combat. This is a grey area, a twilight zone. This is cover and concealment, fire and movement, a pale moon in a grey sky.

This is *Innere Führung* – *Auftragstaktik* – movement as a state – *Über Gräber vorwärts* (and more about these in chapter 4).

This is the astral war, a fight between light and dark. In this fight, there are also vast liminal areas in between. We will now begin to explore this grey threshold and fight for the light. But you can't just say *God, light,* and *Hallelujah* all the time. As a mythopoetic actor and an Actionist, art and ambiguity must also be onboard.

In this vein, I welcome you to the grey area.

This is the fight of the willful warrior against the Demiurge. This is the realm of the saying, I AM. This is the fact that I AM – that I'm a conscious, will-endowed human being, looking, deliberating, and reacting to the environment. No one can stop me from expressing myself. No one can stop me from acknowledging my Soul Spark, my personal fragment of the Divine Light, "*das Vünklein der Seele.*"

In the grey area, I AM. In the borderland, the no man's land, the zone, I AM. In the astral war, I AM.

God created your soul. The soul is energy, and he gave you energy. It is up to you to acknowledge, nurture and enhance that energy. Make your personal energy merge with divine energy.

Your soul is energy. In the energy war, you fight to maintain and increase your energy. You defend your soul, stopping it from being sucked away by the forces of darkness.

This struggle has gone on since the dawn of time. Now, it has become all-pervading, being fought on a virtual battlefield, man's collective consciousness in the era of electronic media. The battlefield is the human consciousness constantly online, constantly hooked to media, and continuously exposed to propaganda. Yes, indeed, this is propaganda, an assault against the soul. Stand armed in this war and realize the fluent character of it. Facts and figures only count in this regarding their symbolic quality. This astral war is primarily fought with timeless symbols, myths, and questions. It is never about modern abstractions like society, the middle class, or democracy. Instead, the elements of this war are symbols like the golden eagle, the silver unicorn, the water of life, and the spear of destiny.

So, I say: ignore the dangers and have your soul sucked away. Instead, be aware of the risks and persevere.

Your soul is the battlefield. *You* are the battlefield. Controlling your will–thought makes you into a Spirit Warrior. Ignoring this makes you into propaganda war cannon fodder.

God created your soul. The soul is energy. The soul is everything: *idam sarvam, yad ayam ātmā.* So, therefore, this mindful war we're in, this energy war, is a total war.

I fight this war. I operate. But the operations aren't as clear-cut as in a material war, a *tangible, boots-on-the-ground, shoot-em-up war.* The energy war is subtler and has another rhythm. It occurs in the astral grey area, in hearts and minds, conceptual and ontological lands. The astral war is fought in this virtual grey area. Therefore, the results are immaterial and intangible, unlike a "real" war, a shooting war. The battlefield of the astral war is your mind.

War in everyday reality is a material war. The astral war is an energy war. We're all soldiers in it, all combatants of it, whether we like it or not. There are no non-combatants, no neutral spaces or forces in it. It is a virtual, mindful case of do-or-die.

Of course, even the real, tangible wars, the shooting wars of our day, are part of the astral war – since the astral dimension permeates everything. Everything has an astral counterpart. "We always sacrifice on altars, even if we're not conscious of it." – Jünger.

No one is neutral in the astral war. It is a total war, and your mind is at stake. In this context, the agent pledging neutrality isn't superior to those taking sides. Even if some may think: "Look at me, I'm so neutral, I'm not led astray by this and that ideology, and therefore I deserve a gold medal of impartiality." Instead, the neutralist is "a soul on vacation." He needs to use his mentality and wake up to reality.

The war is total, and "not taking sides" is also a way of taking sides – the wrong way. Since it is an irresponsible way, in the end, it only benefits the Demiurge.

As I've shown in *Actionism,* we all have to act. No human being stands above reality. We all have to partake in material reality to sustain our bodies. We must take responsibility for our being in both the material and the astral realms.

You are formally allowed not to take sides and pledge ignorance of this and that issue. You won't be struck by lightning if you remain neutral. But please, don't carry your ignorance as a badge of honor.

Then, the quietist-traditionalist operator might say, "but I really am above the hubbub of everyday reality, above the bickering on the internet, for I meditate and seek spiritual tranquility."

Then I'd say, congrats, for then you are at the forefront of the astral war, fighting the rule of the Demiurge, Lord of Darkness, the soul-devouring "Eagle" Castaneda speaks of, the source of the force of mindless materialism harassing us with brainwashing, taxation, and regimentation. However, neutral, you are not. No one is neutral because of the total nature of this war – the astral war, the psychic war – a war where everyone is involved by merely being a conscious human being.

I fight the astral war – against my enemies – the Demiurge and his minions. I'm a Responsible Man, a total man, an action man fighting for the realization of the Midsummer Century.

I fight for truth, will, and passion. *Sac cid ānanda, so 'hām so 'hām.* The enemy fights for debility, desire, and death. The dark side starts wars, and the light sends teachers.

This is where you choose sides. There are no neutral forces and no safe spaces in the astral war.

I'm a Responsible Man, an absolute man, a *Sonnenmensch,* a *vīra,* an astral hero. So, join me today and be the voice of a new generation, fight the astral tyranny, and be free.

Not even God is neutral in the astral war. So, why would you be?

You might think, "God is on the right hand, the Demiurge is on the left, and I am in the middle as the elevated non-committed one."

This is a misconception. Initially, there was primeval Will, who united with primeval Thought. Next, this dyad chose light and became God resplendent, saying "I AM" as a performative statement to seal the deal. The light then started to depolarize primordial darkness, which gave rise to time and motion, symbolized in the Tao symbol. In its rotation, light and dark are not equal – instead, light is the active, spiritual element. At the same time, darkness is reactive and unanimated, only brought along by the light's movement.

This is the astral war. If you choose light, you choose life, creativity, and zest. And if you choose darkness, you choose death, sterility, and ultimate ennui.

There is, of course, an element of "integrating opposites" in any spiritual path – so darkness isn't totally useless. There are vast grey areas in the astral war territory, but to affirm your spiritual being is to choose the light. To deny it is to choose the dark.

There is no neutrality in choosing between the light, the divine side, and the dark, the demiurgic side.

You either affirm that you have an immortal soul, or you deny it.

God created your soul. Your soul is energy. The current fight is a fight about maintaining or being deprived of your energy.

This is the essence of the astral war.

Again: you might say you are no warrior; you are entirely peaceful. But, then I say, to be peaceful is the privilege reserved for those who *know* that they're fighting the astral war, the frequency war, the energy war.

"Non-combatant? Ain't no such thing today," as we have it in *We Were Soldiers*.

Also, we have this Japanese saying, "It is better to be a warrior in a garden than a gardener in a war."

Weaponize your mind...!

3. INTERLUDE

Forwards in the virtual combat zone, movement as a state in the twilight zone... grey men in the grey area, a shadow among shadows, a weed among weeds... a brick in the wall, a rail in the railway, a nail in the coffin... *shadowlands*.

Shadowlands, no man's land, twilight zone, grey area, the middle zone... the borderland.

This is the grey area, the zero point, the basic level, equanimity. Stoic *apatia* and vedic *samatva*.

This is myth, saga, legend. This is divine possession, inspiration, inebriation, initiation. This is revelation in the spirit à la *"Béhemot et Léviathan existent,"* as in Jünger's *Heliopolis*.

Astral war, total war, energy war... inspiration, inebriation, intuition... a re-interpretation, a way to get to know the "I," the Self, the true me.

Fire and movement, constantly on the edge, constantly at storming distance, constantly at the seat perilous... I am the edge, I take control, I am god = *Aham brahmāsmi*.

World as myth. Forward over graves. Empty spaces, what are we living for...

Death of affect as approach to character. Strongpoint defense with a platoon in reserve. It is an ancient mariner, he stoppeth one of three.

German words hard to succinctly translate: *Glaubenskraft* – *Minnesänger* – *Seinsverbundenheit* – *Daseinsbejahung* – *Sonnenmensch* – *Elementarwesen.*

Not hard to translate are these German lines: *Die Wilde Jagd* – *Sieg des Glaubens* – *Tag der Freiheit.*

Let us go out in the grey area, nod at the moon, thrive in this virtual Coventry... Coventry – a special place – as in "to Coventry with you" – neither heaven nor hell, just a nondescript place of exile – or a haven – you just don't know.

It is a tough location, but you have the essentials.

Grey area, borderland, no man's land – Coventry – silent war.

The metaphysical meaning of the current struggle: to find this is the gist of astral war. As are:

- To be the sunshine zeitgeist, a Sonnenmensch, a solar man.
- To be a shaman, occupied with experiments in magical realism.
- "Overcoming the human condition." – Evola

4. WAR AS BEING – THE WARRIOR WAY OF TRUTH

In the previous chapters, I've told you about the astral war. Hereby I present some musings on the role of the *warrior* in this context – how to "be a warrior" in the glorified, moral and spiritual sense, and to be a paragon of responsibility and awareness; a spiritually apt agent in the flurry of existence and beyond, enjoying it to the full.

In *Actionism* (2017), the concept of *Action as Being* was crucial. This remains a focal point of Actionist thought. For example, we all have to act to sustain our bodily functions; we must all breathe. Even thinking is action: the effort of controlled thought entails willpower. "In the beginning was the deed" (Faust). To be is to act, and to act is to be. Here we will discuss *War as Being*, which has the same general meaning as Action as Being – only more warlike and more appropriate in the context of the astral war.

Actionism and even *Borderline* (2015) touched upon this subject – of war as spiritual elevation and the study of soldiering as moral inspiration. However, this chapter aims to grasp the nettle of this subject and deliver some fresh angles.

The main Actionist interest in war is the personal–moral aspect: How to live like a warrior and raise yourself mentally in the process.

One inspiration for this comes from the books of Carlos Castaneda. In these, the guru Don Juan always speaks about becoming a warrior. When asked by the pupil if a warrior can be a role-model for a man of knowledge, Don Juan says that he doesn't speak about war in the sense of destruction and violence. Instead, he speaks about it as a mental elevator.

In other words, the nagualist disciple needs the warrior simile to act as "a moral equivalent of war."

War can bring out the best (and worst) in man. Here we focus on the best qualities: heroism, willpower, possessing the ability to rise to the occasion, and "being all that you can be."

Primarily, a spirit warrior knows about death. Castaneda spoke of this, as did bushido. We also presented this in *Actionism*. The Actionist knows that his physical body has a limited lifespan. This– *Memento Mori Mindset* – makes him calm. His spirit will live on after death.

In *Actionism,* we also spoke of the German military concept of *Verantwortungsfreude* (the joy of responsibility). This entails assuming responsibility gladly, as does a soldier on the battlefield, and, within the framework of the mission at hand, doing everything possible to assure victory.

To thrive while being responsible is the core of Actionism since the very subtitle of *Actionism* is "How to Become a Responsible Man."

In the same context, *Actionism* spoke of another German concept: *Innere Führung* or Inner Leadership. In the Bundeswehr, this means that every solider must be his own chief. For example, when they are idle, they must find a task to occupy themselves with, such as taking care of equipment, chopping wood, or tidying up the cantonment. It does not entail simply awaiting orders like a robot. Within the mission framework, a lot can be done by the ranker's own initiative.

Like Verantwortungsfreude, Inner Leadership is an otherwise established concept capturing the gist of Actionism. Inner equates with thought; Leadership equates with the will. Will-Thought is the basis of man and is the most potent force in the universe, as *Actionism* intimated.

Vernichtungsschlacht is yet another German concept of war that Actionism embraced. This kind of battle is the encirclement, the *Kesselschlacht*, where one of the contestants is surrounded and eradicated as a fighting force. The historical battles of Cannae, Fraustadt, and Tannenberg are examples of this, as are the WWII battles of Suomussalmi and the German eastern front victories of 1941: Minsk, Smolensk, and Kiev. But, details aside, they can be seen as examples of the ultimate artwork. And Actionism, too, has a strain of artistry over it. As in lauding the saying, "the spirit of song is war."

So, whereto, spirit soldier...? Attack, of course. Always attack! Another German proverb for this would be: *Über Gräber vorwärts.* The Hans von Seeckt ideal.

Don't get bogged down in trench warfare; no, get up and go!

Attack, always attack. And trenches or not trenches, this embracing of the attack, of attack as a lifestyle, separates the spiritual soldier from the IRL soldier. An IRL soldier must practice both the attack and the defense. However, the spiritual soldier, the Actionist warrior, is only about the attack. As Serrano says:

> [The spirit warrior must take] ... a path untraveled even by the Gods in all the Ages of this closed Universe. And because the Way does not exist, the hero "makes it on the run," invents it, opens it with the blows of his Sword. [*The Ultimate Avatar*, 2014, p. 376]

In imagining his spirit warrior, Serrano had the Grail knights in mind: Parsifal, King Arthur, and others. It is a fine symbol for the Actionist warrior: a noble, spiritual fighter, using the business of combat as a means for spiritual elevation and moral perfection. Having the Grail knight as an ideal, along with Castaneda's "Indian Warrior" archetype, will illustrate what "fighting as being" in the Actionist sense is all about.

The gist of the spirit warrior is this: forever living as if amid battle, embodying fierce and hectic action, but not letting this affect you nor succumbing to stress. Instead, the mere presence of action calms you. Thus, you are forever living in *apatia, sang-froid, samatva,* and equanimity – living in total concentration and relaxation, indifferent to happiness and sorrow: *sukha–duḥkha–samā*, eternally enjoying the emptiness of the moment, the nothingness now – all this while acting.

War as Being is about attack, always attack. Coolness and restraint must be remembered, but generally, the spirit warrior is about being strong and powerful – fighting bravely in the offensive mode is the primary symbol of this.

No immortal hero ever won battles by being locked in a fortress.

This is about the "triumph of the will to immortality."

This is about "fire and movement as spiritual elevation."

This is about the central Actionist tenets of "Movement as a State" and "Rest in Action" – to always be active but not striving to reach a conclusion, instead it is the very state of being active you strive for. *Actionism* explained that in discussing Rest in Action.

The poet Karin Boye wrote about this elevated state of the warrior: "Rest only awaits you in battle. Only between the shields there is peace."

A similar Swedish Valkyrie poet was Edith Södergran, who stated that "the spirit of song is war." She lauded war as an aesthetic, elementary action. "War" in her hands became truly mythical in the astral sense. For instance, she wrote about the hero being "enraptured in tranquility," following his path with "*amor fati*" inscribed on his banner, discarding everything having to do with "slow," "careful," and "try." (More about Södergran's fiery poetry can be found in *Borderline*.)

This is *devotion* in the original Roman sense: to put your life in God's hands and fight without a thought of tomorrow. *Devotio,* as it was called in Latin. The Actionist is devoted in this sense: to affirming the inner, divine light vigorously.

This is war as being. This is a constant attack. This is Odin, the God of war, poetry, and ecstasy...

This is the Grail. This is Kalki on a white horse:

> And I looked, and behold, a white horse. He who sat on it had a bow; and a crown was given to him, and he went out conquering and to conquer. [Rev. 6:2]

This is spirit war, astral war, and total war in the spiritual sense. Your soul is the battlefield. Go to this war with a song on your lips: "the spirit of song is war."

So, prepare for total war: a total, absolute, all–out war against materialism. As I said in a poem published in a rather recent anthology [Finlayson Taylor, 2019]:

> I am the Holy Flame,
>
> I am the Holy Fire...
>
> I am the flash in the firepan,
>
> fire and movement preaching man.
>
> Burning all materialism to ashes.
>
> I will burn it to ashes, then burn the ashes.

In other words, it will be the ultimate *Vernichtungsschlacht*.

Attack. You must attack. Schlieffen: "Without an attack, the enemy can't be beaten." He meant this is the very fundament of the art of war.

That doesn't mean that one should sit behind a desk and command destruction via mechanical means. Having "no face, no name, just a killing machine" is just an anonymous internet poster playing wargames, spewing bile in online debates.

No way...! Instead, the Actionist idea of War as Being implies that you state your name openly, like an old-school knight, before battle and then fight.

You must act openly in the astral, electronic, or propaganda wars. You can't hide behind a pseudonym forever. You can't just sit there and make wry faces at your computer when you see things you don't like. You can't just make anonymous comments.

If you want to ascend or be a human operator in the Actionist sense, you must state your name during debates and say, "I don't approve of this."

You must have a face and a name. You must be yourself. The I AM dictum must be weaponized.

But doesn't openly stating your name expose you unnecessarily?

Yes. But "without an attack, the enemy can't be beaten."

You don't always have to seek conflict in discussions actively, but, as I will explain later, you must make some form of debating debut, even if it is only stating your metaphysical beliefs. In the current zeitgeist, everything is controversial. Nothing is uncontroversial. You must speak your mind openly and without caveats.

The Powers That Be (TPTB) want to dehumanize all adversaries in the current struggle. Therefore, you need to be "a human operator." This entails stating when you oppose the regime.

Having the I AM ingrained in his being, in and out of battle, an Actionist is the opposite of "the man of the crowd" (who, for his part, was portrayed in *Actionism*, Chapter 32).

As intimated previously, Södergran said, "the spirit of song is war." This is an Odinic statement, given that Odin was the God of war and poetry. Södergran (and Boye) had this Valkyrie aspect. The racial memory goes deep. (More of "the odic power" in Chapter 11).

"There are vast grey areas in the astral war territory."

For, while I am all for the light and don't peddle a dark agenda *per se*, you also have to acknowledge the grey area of the astral war. You fight and have allies of the "spiritual friendship" kind. And while it is good to have allies, it must be remembered that the atmosphere of this existence is "cold." Not unfriendly cold, but it isn't warm like the existence of the mindless mundane-reality kind, living like a collective soul in the ethereal-material sphere (like being "a member of family X," "an employee of company Y," "a fan of football team Z" etc.). The astral sphere is above this, and so the astral reality can be a bit trying – for those not used to living mindfully.

You'll get used to it after a while, though. Practice makes perfect. You'll be a virtual Aeon Flux saying to yourself, "I am the edge"...

"Watcher, what of the night?"

I'll tell you, watcher of the skies and watcher of the earth, watcher of the water and watcher of fire: night draws to a close, and the day is dawning. Behold, it is a new day, so take out your instruments and play – play the song of astral war, fire, and movement, baptism of fire – of assaying the soul, testing the heart – of walking the Sirat Bridge, dancing over it if you know how to do it. You know how to operate astrally. Let intuition guide you.

Initiation, inebriation, and intuition are the leitmotif. That is an initiation by birth, not secret rituals; inebriation, from art, culture, music; intuition, to let your sixth sense guide you.

This is the era of intuition; match the platform or to Coventry with you, away with you to the hologram, to the illusionary set-up where you and yours can continue to live out your dualistic mindset until you've learned better. "Let us have done with you, you rogues!"

In Chapter 2, I said, "forwards in the virtual combat zone." And in the astral war, it is all about going forward and attacking.

Of course, you have to rein it in somewhat. Don't foolhardily rush into any "frequency war situations." However, the proficient astral warrior exists in a state of perpetual attack. It is his way of life, the state of living to fight, fighting to live. He fights his way, creating it as he goes, the same way as an Aboriginal in the Dreaming sings forth his way as he goes. Astral warriors move along dreamlines.

Astral war is a grey area war. I personally participated in the "cold war," a real grey area war if there ever was one. But, of course, there is something unfulfilling in this "waiting game" type of war, for this (from a Swedish point of view) entailed "never deploying the units for real, always practicing, no bloodletting, eternal Sitzkrieg, eternal Phoney war." Even so, I won't go into the details of "the not-doings of the cold war."

However, in defense of the cold war, it came with a very war-like state of mind. Serving in the Swedish army in 1984-85 was comparatively more severe than doing it ten years later, after the end of the cold war. In 1984 the mindset, "the strategic subconscious," was about expecting a Bolshevik surprise attack any day, 24/7; ten years later, that threat was no more. In 1984, the war sentiment was tangible due to the massive amounts of battle–ready Soviet units deployed on the other side of the Baltic Sea.

Thus, I can cherish the "virtual state of war" about this experience. It was the best possible training ground imaginable for an astral warrior.

In the context of astral war, publishing a book is a strategic feat. A published book is a magical act, its inherent power being "beyond good and evil."

This is the grey area. And this is the grey *era* – a temporal nexus of everything, an era promising everything, yet, an era that isn't bristling in colors at the moment. A bit nondescript, a bit grey – soberly grey. "Fade to Grey" by Visage would be a fine soundtrack for these times – the time of the grey area, the borderland, the No Man's Land.

This is the astral war, the magic war, the spirit war – the invisible war, the secret war – the frequency war, the energy war, the holy war, the total war. Your soul is the battlefield. Anyone endowed with a soul is drawn in. No one is neutral in this virtual war, a war going on from the dawn of time, now and forever – as long as there will be light and dark, God and Demiurge, Devas and Asuras, men and women.

Here is a pertinent astral war quote from Yukio Mishima's novel *Runaway Horses* (1969):

> If we look on idly, heaven and earth will never be joined. To join heaven and earth, some decisive deed of purity is necessary. To accomplish so resolute an action, you have to stake your life, giving no thought to personal gain or loss. You have to turn into a dragon and stir up a whirlwind, tear the dark, brooding clouds asunder and soar up into the azure–blue sky.

And, from the same book: "Perfect purity is possible if you turn your life into a line of poetry, written with a splash of blood." This is the essence of the astral war: conceptualizing your whole life into art.

The astral war is an invisible war, a war for your soul: your soul is the battlefield. And since "the soul is everything" – *idam sarvam, yad ayam ātmā* – it is also a total war.

This is the astral war equation. No one is neutral. Everyone is taking part in it, whether he knows it or not. The only choice is between being a victim or a victor.

Thus, a scared soul expecting a global nuclear war equals "an astral war victim." On the other hand, a calm soul, having willpower control over his emotions, equals "an astral war winner."

The astral war is a total war. Therefore, it must end with unconditional surrender for the losing side. You must harbor no illusions of "communication across the frontlines," of virtual "football games in no man's land at Christmas" – for the trenches are dug deep. Instead, prepare for virtual Vernichtungsschlacht.

However, you must not take this as a *carte blanche* to become a mindless titan, a laughing demon, or a slaughterer. Maintain your humanity. But in all other respects, prepare for psychic war—a long, total one.

Standing with one foot on Mars and one foot on Venus, I say: turn away from materialism and start building *Antropolis*, the first human civilization dedicated to art, science, and spirituality.

In the propaganda war raging 24/7, the personal goal is to be "a great general in dreamland," not a soldier in the trenches.

Of course, trench-fighting is operationally needed for victory – but – take a look at yourself when you are online. Are you always "fighting the troll," or are you taking care of your own soul, operating in a way you like...?

"A good tactic is one that your people enjoy," as it reads in *Rules for Radicals.*

The personal reconquista (q.v. Philippe Vardon) demands that you publicly make a stand, even if only on social media. You have to make a debating debut. In fighting for freedom, you can't go on being a conceptual virgin, forever sitting on the fence, giving each his due. You must leave the conceptual closet. You must fight the metapolitical fight. And be prepared for bruises. For,

> The inferior man argues about his rights, while the superior man imposes duties on himself.
> – Wagner Clemente Soto

I declare you the spiritual superman. Materialist man is something to be overcome.

> The future is what is created through the will; only the one who wills has a future.
> – Otto Weininger

You have been living in an era of reductive science and machine technology. That era is about to end. Now we're entering a period of spiritual science and spiritualized technology.

It is about integration, psycho-synthesis (and not psychanalysis), wave physics (and not particle physics), and holistic mathematics *à la* Pythagoras (and not algebra).

It is about integrative holism, not divisive reductionism.

Reductionist science is 3D, third density, the material world. Conversely, spiritual science is 4D, fourth density, the astral world.

The Astral war slogan is: Make love *and* war. This has a mythical justification: Mars was the lover of Venus, and they had the son Cupid aka Amor.

Yet, I have not come to bring peace. Instead, I bring you astral war and strife. And you should love the long astral war more than the short. For what warrior wants to be spared?

Go forth to the astral battlefield, armed with Will-Thought, and emerge triumphant. Neglect it and be devoured by the Demiurge, the Thousand Year Dragon, the Black Eagle, the Blind Idiot God writhing at the heart of the cosmos to the monotonous piping of a demonic flute.

Sum up your Will-Thought and fortify your soul... or else it will be sucked away by the Great Cthulhu.

I have not come to promulgate peace. The Astral War rages strong. It has been raging since the dawn of time, since the beginning of materiality, since souls incarnated as flesh. Since then, light and dark have struggled, and man's soul is the battlefield.

Acknowledge your soul's essential light and strive for divinity or be embroiled in matter and worship the Demiurge.

You choose.

There is no neutral faction in this war.

Everybody wants to be in my crowd – the Actionist crowd.

You can see us at forest edges at twilight, gliding down endless hallways, or at firing ranges, measuring the distance from here to eternity.

Read *Borderline* and *Actionism* and join us. We will recognize each other when we meet.

The astral war is energy, action, myth, symbol, and revelation. You must master myth and revelation, energy and action, to survive.

Commandments of the Astral Warrior

- *I am free* – not by some political decision; freedom is my property by birth, by being a will-endowed, thinking human being.

- *I am free* because I am responsible for everything that I do.

- *I am free* because I AM.

Explanation and deliberation: the astral warrior has his freedom inborn; no one can take it away from him, for it is his by birthright. Freedom, as in "freedom of thought, freedom of speech, academic freedom, artistic freedom," is ingrained into his being. Conversely, without these fundamental freedoms, we possess nothing, only serfdom and slavery.

The astral warrior is free. His will leads him on. And will, by definition, is free (the opposite of "will" is "desire").

The astral warrior's will is fused with his thought into will-thought; this is his very being, and this interacts with his passion and vision.

Otherwise, listing what characterizes an astral warrior is rather useless. He merely says, "I AM," *und so ist alles gesagt.* "I AM" is the formula for "life, universe, and everything." And, as Evola underlines in *Ride the Tiger:* intelligent people find their morality by intuition; there is no need for any ten commandments or noble eightfold paths. I am free, and you are free; let us not infringe on each other's freedoms; otherwise, a will-endowed, thinking human doesn't need detailed moral instructions.

I am an Astral Warrior. I weaponize my will, thought, and passion. I am weaponized mindfulness.

I'm an Astral Warrior, in and out of this army and that. For instance, in fighting the Cold War, I was mustered by the Swedish army authorities in 1983. I served as an infantryman from 1984-1985. In 2000 I was discharged; my services weren't needed anymore. That was part of the large cutting-down of the Swedish army post-Cold War. My soldiery life was virtually over. I was "called to the Great Army" – *zum grossen Armee gerufen* – recruited into the Astral Army, the Wild Hunt, *das Wilde Heer* of Odin. And in this, I still fight tirelessly, fighting for truth and light, fighting evil, fighting to gain positive power, forever "on the move," constantly attacking, always in "movement as a state of mind."

I'm courteous to people that I meet. I give everyone his due. But if anyone puts his hand on me, I will defend myself.

> The most powerful weapon on earth is the
> human soul on fire.
> – Ferdinand Foch

I don't dig trenches. I operate with spiritual fire and movement.

If you don't have any enemies, get some. It will validate you.

5. HOLISM

The astral war is a holistic concept. Holism is the opposite of reductionism, the current *Leitkultur* of the West. Here we present a brief summary of holism, providing a comprehensive description of it and all that it stands for.

Firstly, let's explore holism from the opposite perspective: what holism is *not*. And that is *reductionism*. In natural science, "reductionism" entails deconstructing reality into what you can study in a laboratory, fragmenting reality into observable bits and pieces. This attitude may answer limited questions. However, it can't be construed as a metaphysical worldview, a philosophy of being, or an ontology.

Thus, the error of reductionism is *making methodological reduction into ontological reduction.* One doesn't follow the other. Therefore, scientific reductionism is a viable method only to study some aspects of physical reality.

As such, Actionism doesn't discard the modern scientific method.

For example, the "periodic table of elements" is still valuable for examining physical reality. However, it still has its limits. You can't reduce complex organisms into just hydrogen, oxygen, and nitrogen. Organisms aren't shaped by elements *per se*; they are shaped by ideas – Greek, *eidoi*.

We must elevate ourselves above physical reductionism to reach a more comprehensive, fully-rounded worldview.

We need to go *from reductionism to a systemic vision.* To holism so that we can perceive the whole and the Big Picture.

It is not just the life sciences that need to be elevated into holism. The same applies to the humanities.

Thus, the time is up for social theories to reduce man into an eating, sleeping, and fornicating animal. The time is up for medicine and psychology to reduce man into a machine that can only be cured with surgical procedures and drugs. The time is up for social science to see man as an unwritten thesis that propaganda can manipulate. The time is up to reduce "rule by law" to the existence of written law paragraphs, discarding the eternal existence of moral values. The time is up for biographies reducing authorship to what the author materially experienced in life, concentrating all his life and art into temporal, contingent nonsense.

In other words, *the time of reductionism is over*. Man isn't a machine, a vessel fed by food and drink. With his inner mind, he is in contact with the invisible side of reality, the *noosphere*, the world of ideas and eternal concepts such as will, truth, and compassion, from which everything else is derived – courage, fidelity, justice, faith, and magnanimity.

We need a more complex view of man and nature, a more differentiated view, not the dualist pattern of real/unreal, true/false, and good/bad that reductionism leads to. We need an organic look at science, taking every aspect in, not a binary computer-style attitude. Organisms work holistically, while machines work serially. That is the main difference.

And I'd say even today's mainstream "school" science has this holistic attitude implied, like an embryo of a new paradigm. Modern science fully knows how Archimedes, seemingly out of the blue, found the principle of buoyancy – by "just getting it," saying *eureka* – I've found it. It knows of Francis Crick getting the vision of the DNA double helix while in a trance. It knows of Stradonitz dreaming of a snake biting its tail, leading him to the concept of the benzene ring structure.

Thus, science can't just observe material reality. A scientist must also look inside himself – *"in homine interior habitat veritas."* Truth is an inner phenomenon, virtually, an esoteric thing (not an exoteric, outer thing). By introspection, man can discover eternal truths using the sixth sense, the inner eye, and the pineal gland. Holistic, essential impulses are gained by going inside and encountering the *eidos* unmitigated.

That is the esoteric, holistic attitude of Actionism. And with the marriage of outer observation and inner contemplation, a new science will be born.

6. SOME REMARKS ABOUT GOD

Discussing God is like discussing gold – meaningless. You are either moved by it or not. As symbols of "the best, the highest, the essential," they simply *are*.

However, some remarks on the subject of God can be offered to provide a background for the current astral war discussion. Below I will venture out into that impossible grey area of trying to conceptualize God. As always, the Actionist attitude is implied.

"The chief purpose of life... is to increase according to our capacity our knowledge of God by all the means we have, and to be moved by it to promise and thanks."

J.R.R. Tolkien wrote this. It sums up the feeling of one who believes in God very well.

While Actionism isn't primarily devotional like Tolkien's attitude, it excludes such sentiment. As shown in *Borderline* and *Actionism*, the Actionist concept of God is in the realm of "I have the divine light within," "ye are gods," and such. But – an individual, human god believer, feeling "god inside," being able to say "*aham brahmāsmi* (I am god)," of course, isn't above God. God has created man, but man hasn't created God. Thus, a little devotion, like that of Tolkien above, is pertinent for an Actionist and all divinely inclined people.

Tolkien was moved to gratitude by God. But, Contrariwise, the lack of having someone to thank in this way defines the atheist: "The worst moment for the atheist is when he is really thankful and has nobody to thank," as Dante Gabriel Rossetti said.

In order to illuminate this complex concept, we may focus on its opposite for a while, atheism, the stance of denying God.

So, what can be said about atheism from an Actionist point of view? This quote from an unknown source sums it up: "When people stop believing in God, they don't believe in nothing – they believe in anything!" Atheism isn't just "another worldview," along with theism and agnosticism. The only viable atheism is the ontological, "Buddhist" one, even though it discards elements like "an eternal soul." However, in Buddhism, you nonetheless lead a life of awe, wonder, piety, and kindness. Not that ordinary atheists can't be kind – but their claim of being above the essential reality sets them apart. The delusion that they think they can explain away God, the source of reality, just like that.

You cannot get around the concept of God. But, of course, you can be anti-clerical and attack the external aspect of religion, such as church and priesthood. Even St. Paul and Luther did that, advocating "the universal priesthood" where every conscious individual becomes his own priest in his personal relation to God. However, you have no ontological right to discard the existence of a supreme force, a supreme source for reality – for everything.

Being in the grey area of agnosticism is better than being so sure of the non-existence of God.

Do you, as an individual, think you can triumph over creation?

A man is just "another being in reality," another *Seiendes im Sein.* He can't place himself above Sein merely with some casuistry. This was covered in *Borderline.*

Atheism is the scourge of our times.

I suspect people become atheists because of a lack of intuition, their consciousness afflicted with a disconnection to the invisible aspect of reality, lacking the ability to harmonize with their inner depths.

For its part, atheist materialism abounds in late–period societies past their prime. For example, ancient Rome and India had the same issues with stoicism, epicureanism, and *carvaka.* But perennial tradition (whereof Actionism is a part) conquers all, conveying this eternal truth.

So, where does this take us? I will end where I began, in quietly acknowledging God.

Shirley MacLaine described the nature of God as a "Divine God Intelligence Field." This is reminiscent of Philip K. Dick's theophany, leading him to call the divine force in his life a "Vast Active Life Improvement System." His divine "1974 experience" was beneficial in the end, but it was also harrowing and trying, which I have covered in my book *Science Fiction Seen from the Right*.

As stated previously (*aham brahmāsmi*, "I am God"), an individual has the divine inside of him. A man is a "god in being" created by the eternal light, with a fragment of this eternal light inside. You could say that a man is a god because of (1) having an eternal soul, (2) having specific bodily proportions, being created in god's image. This means: to be a god in physicality, a physical angel. "A man is a mortal god; a god is an immortal man." – Herakleitos.

Having the divine approach in life is about seeing the invisible, beyond the Beyond, and beyond the conditioned. To fathom the unfathomable.

And faith is both to *fall down* in amazement before the wonders of the cosmos – and to *elevate* yourself above the blandness of everyday reality. "When I'm down on my knees, that's when I'm closest to Heaven" and "humble pride," as the Prophet said, is a fine oxymoron; being aware of your shortcomings as a human being but nonetheless feeling pride over what a man can accomplish. Man is "a god in being." "God–realization" is man's most noble goal.

God is more than you can grasp mentally. But you can still be conscious of the immanent presence of God. This means having *god-consciousness*.

Therefore, the gist of Actionism is divine and spiritual.

Essentially, Actionism is about seeking the Holy Grail. The epic of Actionism is Parsifal reaching an understanding of cosmic integration, comprising not only the healing of the ailing king but also the restoration of the spiritual kingdom of man.

Actionism is unity, holism, integration – not divisiveness, dissection, "critical theory" masticating everything and vomiting forth bile. Actionism, on the contrary, is concerned with spiritual gold.

Actionism provides a heavenly approach, and flawless integration with the divinely meaningful world: God-bred, spirit-led, inspiration-fed.

This is the worldview of God-given insights, inner voice, and divine providence.

This is the world of the individual having a personal relation to God.

This is the world of believing in God: *spera in deo.*

This is the world of the individual, acknowledging his inner light – the eternal light. *Lux aeterna.*

Actionism is theistic. One cannot avoid the concept of God. Being 'anti-clerical, anti-Christianity' is one thing; however, denying God and regarding atheism as a proven fact is an entirely different thing. That is madness.

Actionism is, like St. John, in *Getsemaneh*-style: "God and I are one. His life is mine; my life is his. My work is his work, and his work my work."

7. TURNING YOUR LIFE INTO ART

The astral war needs mindful and artistic combatants. In this chapter, I will try to conceptualize the artistic element as an integral part of the "Actionist" astral war experience. The name for this "spiritual aestheticism," this "mythopoetic approach to life," will be *Golden Yoga*.

A. *Setting the Scene*

Let's start with a quote from Richard Wagner, one of the greatest composers in history. I wrote a biography on him in 2015 but did not include the following citation in it. However, it is a fine summation of art-as-religion:

> I believe in God, Mozart, and Beethoven, and likewise their disciples and apostles; – I believe in the Holy Spirit and the truth of the one, indivisible Art; – I believe that this Art proceeds from God, and lives within the hearts of all illumined men; – I believe that he who once has bathed in the sublime delights of this high Art, is consecrate to Her forever, and never can deny Her; – I believe that through Art all men are saved.

Art is essential to man's existence. Art is imbued in the creation. Plotinus (q.v. *Borderline*) believed that creation itself is a beautiful artwork and that artists approach that essential beauty when they create.

This attitude to art, that of the artist as an entranced revealer of metaphysical truth, has lived on in the Western world ever since Plotinus, in the thought of Goethe and Schelling, for example. The latter spoke of "aesthetic intuition," and this is something an Actionist must possess. He must not ignore the power of intuition anywhere, including the realm of art. Art, Actionism, and Golden Yoga are about having a *Dreamer's Description* of the world. Apply this, and everything becomes free and fluid. "Dream-dream-dream and the colors will come naturally..."

I am talking about the Dreamer's Description of the world. Of the esoteric worldview, and the astral worldview, all with an artistic tinge.

It is about willfully going into the land of dreams and legends, stories, and fairy tales. It is about consciously making contact with the astral world.

If you spontaneously can relate to this, then you are on the way to artistic craftsmanship.

To create art, apart from some basic talent, you must have aesthetic intuition, be able to daydream systematically (as Baudelaire said), and just let the creativity flow. Be open. "When I'm closed I am Brion Gysin; when I am open I am the artist" as the author Brion Gysin said.

Previously in this book, I quoted Mishima and his idea of "turning your life into a line of poetry." For its part, this stage is reached by the artist if he has been in the game long enough. Then it comes naturally. Having spent a lifetime stylizing his art, this soon leads to a stylization of himself.

A great self-stylizer in this vein was Nietzsche. Write to live, live to write. The two are inseparable. The same may be seen in the life and work of Ernst Jünger, whom I wrote about in my 2014 biography. I also spoke more about Nietzsche in *Borderline*.

God created the world with willpower and vision. And the artist creates his work with willpower and vision. And the Actionist creates his life with willpower and vision.

Willpower is the leading, active element. Vision is the passive element. As such, vision is akin to thought. Will and Thought are the basics of Actionist metaphysics, as shown in the 2017 book. There is no conflict between will and reason in the Actionist system. In fact, they make a great couple, the strongest force in the universe, when merged in Actionist fashion.

Will and thought, will and vision. You have to merge will with this passive-yet-essential side of things. Do it and become invincible.

Will and vision, a clarification... For example, I *see* before me a bright future; now I *want* it to become reality.

That is the gist of "willpower and vision." In artistic terms: I see before me this artwork (novel, picture, even "my life lived as an artwork"). And, with my will, I realize it. I make it real, and I implement it into tangible reality. All it takes is constant meditation on the mantra, "willpower and vision."

B. The 2017 Document

Actionism – How to Become a Responsible Man is the basic document of Actionism; I refer to it as "the 2017 book." In that book, I spoke about art and "living your life like a work of art." In Chapter 3, I spoke of transforming "acting into an art" and acting like an artist in a trance: "Anchored in being, the Actionist performs actions. As an artist, he operates as if in a trance, seeking rest in action and peace in performing." [Svensson 2017 p. 32]

In the same chapter, I spoke of ennobling "every act, turning away from its immediately material purpose and making action into a *l'art-pour-l'art.*" [ibid p. 34] "The Actionist makes action into an art, a way of life." [p. 37]

This makes you think of "the way is the goal, the action is its own reward." Having an artistic attitude to everything helps to achieve this mode of life.

Next, in Chapter 8, there is "Actionist Art," which spoke of three aspects clarifying what Actionist Art is: vision, musicality, and symbol. Regarding *vision,* this is what an artist does:

> He sees something with his inner eye, then he realizes the vision to the public. Ideally,

an artist is a pathfinder for man, a guide into future vistas. This is conceptualized as "artistic vision is the avantgarde of man" = art must go before everyday reality, as a glorified scouting patrol = art can envision things that "are not real" but in time may become real. [p. 61]

Next, on *music,* I stated, "Without music, life would be a mistake" (Nietzsche) and spoke of *the need for mixing a little musicality into one's stringency.* In this vein, I thought of the following: in the old Russian Empire, *the ability to play a musical instrument* was considered beneficial to a governmental official's general competence.

Finally, in Chapter 8, I spoke of *symbols.* The artist is a visionary because of his ability to see the true nature of things, and their *eidoi*, thus having "an advantage over the common man who only sees the ephemeral and the subjective." [p. 62–63] Goethe, for his part, meant that he could see the *eidos* directly. Goethe was portrayed in *Borderline,* and his esoteric ability, in science and art, remains an inspiring gestalt of Actionism.

C. Art as a Way of Wisdom

You say: avoid excess, remain sane...!

I say: anything worth doing is worth overdoing. *Atasthalía...!*

I say: as an artist, you're basically fighting elemental forces, fighting chaos, and then you have to mobilize every power at your command. You struggle to provide a form for the chaos of images besetting you.

As for remaining sane... okay, this is true, but willpower must be in charge, excess should be avoided in your everyday routines and practices – but otherwise, it is all about burning magnesium, fire and movement, hubris and megalomania, fanaticism and hysteria...!

Don't lecture me about what works and what doesn't. I tread a fine line between the ridiculous and the sublime, and I know it. The only thing carrying me through is *wanting* to be carried through – wanting to succeed – wanting to complete the task at hand. I do, I overdo; then some sane deliberation will have to sort it out. But only when the work is done. To deliberate too much before the event leads nowhere.

You can't plan a perfect artwork in every detail. After the initial framework is sketched out, you have to get going and shape the whole thing.

You say: write about fine, edifying stuff. Don't worship war and death; worship life...!

To this, I reply: it is true that you must have ideals. I am one of the few mindful authors out there today, mindful with an artistic tinge. And that artistic attitude mustn't be quelled by overriding commands of the "write edifying stuff, educate the reader, enlighten the world" kind...

I would rather burn down the world than write a text that is sane and perfect from some cerebral, rational point of view.

The aestheticism of the late 19th century had its merit: the rebellion of the soul against the spirit; to be a sleepwalker led by Providence; the inner voice and inner lantern must lead the way. Remain to stay sane but do also allow yourself to be governed by invisible forces. Then you'll succeed.

This is the artist's commandment, now and forever.

And this strain was seen in writers like Wilde, George, and Nietzsche.

> Art unites and science disconnects. Art gives form to things, science dissects.
> – H. S. Chamberlain, *Foundations of the Nineteenth Century*, Vol. I, Introduction, p. lx

This whole artistic lifestyle, this artistic philosophy of life, this "art as a way of wisdom," and this creative attitude, guided by inner light and intuition – can be, as I said, called *Golden Yoga.*

Golden Yoga implies an artistic approach to life and everything. It is the Actionist yoga, the Actionist way. It is a spiritual alchemy mixing fire and movement, will and thought.

Golden Yoga is about art as life and life as art. It is about expressing thought in symbolic form. Philosophy has to possess an enduring and alluring artistic form.

In the spirit of Alice Bailey, Golden Yoga is about reaching "harmony through conflict." The artwork is a paragon of harmony – but – in order to reach it, you have to stage a conflict. This, then, is the alchemy of Golden Yoga, how to make spiritual gold...!

D. Some Words on Nietzsche

In this chapter, Nietzsche is mentioned several times. He was a philosopher who understood one aspect of Golden Yoga, the need for style, the strain of *life as art and art as life*, and the need for *Selbst-stilisierung* (self-stylization).

This touches on Nietzsche's existential approach: letting your life be an embodiment of what you advocate, letting your being reflect your thought; being and thought are the same in his opus. In other existential thinkers (Kierkegaard, Heidegger, Weil, Sartre), we see the *stylistic will* and the "will to style" (Ger. *Stilwille*). The true artist *is* his artwork, and the true philosopher *is* his opus. He must express himself in a style reflecting his unique being. He must have the will to express himself; he can't write for the academy in ordered periods and passages; he must use any mode of expression to utter his own conceptual-cum-existential vision. This will lead him into art – and out of the academy.

Case in point: in Nietzsche's first work, *Geburt der Tragödie,* he construed a possibly fanciful but workable juxtaposition of Apollonian and Dionysian attitudes, said to have existed in antiquity; however, Nietzsche doesn't support his thesis with ordinary research, he supports it with style.

L'homme et la style, c'est la même... le philosophe et la style, c'est la même.

E. Symbolism

Golden Yoga is "art as a creed." And for creating art, you need symbols. Hereby we present a deliberation on *symbols and symbolism.*

In Thoth's Emerald Tablets, XIV, we read this on symbols: "Hidden in darkness, veiled in symbols, // always the way to the portal will be found."

Symbolism, expressed in nuce: the thing becomes a symbol when *being* shines through.

Mankind expresses itself symbolically. Energy patterns in its mind are projected into architecture, art, religion, politics, and everything else. The mind of man is symbolically projected into tangibly visible creations.

Robert Graves, speaking on symbolism, writes that:

> Symbolism or allegory is 'truer' than realism in that the former allows more possibilities or interpretations. And more possibilities—implying greater freedom and less context dependence—translate to a greater truth. Accordingly, it has been said, 'The more numerous the poetic meanings that could be concentrated in a sacred name; the greater was its power.' [quoted after the foreword of translator Christopher Jones in Otto Rahn, *Crusade Against the Grail.* Rochester, Vermont: Inner Traditions 2006] [Jones adds after quote: "In this way, the Grāl is perhaps the most powerful symbol of all for a simple reason: nobody has ever seen it."]

Concerning symbolism, Rudolf Steiner in *Atlantis and Lemuria* (1904, states that the Atlanteans were not thinking in ideas and abstract concepts but in tangible images and visions:

> The man of the present day has the advantage over the Atlantean of possessing a logical understanding and an aptitude for combination; but on the other hand his memory power has waned. We now think in ideas, the Atlantean thought in pictures; and when a picture rose in his mind he remembered many other similar pictures which he had formerly seen, and then formed his judgment accordingly. Consequently all education then was quite different from that of later times. It was not intended to provide the child with rules or to sharpen his wits. Rather was life presented to him in comprehensive pictures, so that subsequently he could call to remembrance as much as possible, when dealing with this or that circumstance.

It is like hieroglyphic writing or ideograms. Communicating not with abstractions but with relatable symbols. As is the case with Jünger and myself.

The gist of symbolism is captured by Andrei Tarkovsky: "A poet is someone who uses a single image to express a universal message."

It is about the *adamitic* view of language: unity between the thing and the thought. Thus it was in the time of Adam. It is similar to William Carlos

Williams's sentiment: "no thought except in things; say it!"

F. Actionism Always

Myth, math, and metaphor symbolize creativity as a way of life, as a way of transcendence – that is, Golden Yoga, the theme for this section – and on the subject of Golden Yoga, I have more, a lot more to say.

Golden Yoga is the esoteric worldview, the astral worldview, with an artistic tinge.

Golden Yoga is an artistic approach to life and everything. It is the Actionist yoga, the Actionist way. A spiritual alchemy mixing fire and movement, will and thought.

Actionism, actionism always...!

That's my motto. A motto for the strong life, the responsible life.

This is my creed, my philosophy. It is about Actionism. It is about energy, action, toughness, and rigorism.

It is about elitism, supermanism, *superomismo*... to raise yourself and become something more than you are... "be all that you can be," as the US Army slogan said.

I'm heroic and godly. I live the authentic life, the real life, the responsible life – the shiny, radiant, creative, Faustian-heroic life...

I bestow sight and touch with meaning. Everything I say is revelation, everything I do is revelation; everything I see is the *eidos,* the idea, the essence.

I'm a man, a physical body needing fuel and sleep... but in that body, a soul is also dwelling, a refined soul possessed of the divine spark. That's what makes me divine.

You could say that I'm a god, lowercase g, acknowledging the higher God.

I face up to everything I can, I even master it: life and death, fear and superstition. I control every thought, every emotion, every muscle, every nerve...

I'm a self-ordained god-man, realizing I have God within.

G. Diverse

"The only rule governing creativity is the act of creation itself" (Frank Herbert, *Children of Dune*, p. 354, NEL 1984)... the only purpose of an artwork is to prove that it could be done.

Heart of gold, Golden Yoga...

Golden yoga is a spiritual aestheticism.

I'm an example of the aesthetic-heroic man, untouched by critical reason.

God bless piety and esotericism – but – a wholly pious man can't create art. An artist has to be ruthless; he must be true to his vision. In the same way, an all too prudent and perfect woman isn't sexy. She needs to be a little dirty if only marginally, to have some sexual allure. 100% piety is the death of art.

H. Nordic Midsummer Night

Earlier, I referred to Tarkovsky and the artist himself morphing into a work of art. This will bring the chapter to a satisfying conclusion by exploring the phenomenon at the intersection between life, ethics, ontology, and art.

The quote we now will examine concerns Tarkovsky's 1985 film *The Sacrifice.*

The scene is the villa, the country house. In the never-ending Nordic midsummer night, the medical doctor, Victor, and some friends are sitting by a table out in the open. And at 1.32-1.33 he says the following:

> As I understood Alexander's words, he meant that it is peculiar for a man, to change, of his own free will, into a work of art. Generally, the result of all poetic striving lies so far from its author that one can hardly believe that it is a man-made creation. In the case of the actor, though, the reverse is true. The actor is, himself, his own creation, his own work of art.

As I understand this statement, an actor (or an artist conscious of his worth) unifies immanence with transcendence. The artwork is an almost supernatural occurrence; something transcendent is revealed inside himself, in his earthly, bodily form – in something immanent.

He is a living wonder, a one-man university, a wonder revealed... everything he does becomes myth, legend, Holy Writ. Everything he touches becomes gold.

8. QUINTA ESSENTIA

This book is about *the Astral War*. A war in which your soul is the battlefield. A mindful war where you need mindful ammunition to flourish.

It is an energy war where the ammunition used is *mental energy*. And *mental energy* is a subject that has always been part of Actionism.

I mentioned mental energy in Chapters 2, 4, and 32 of *Actionism* (2017); for instance, I spoke of "saving mental energy." It meant that inside of you, there is a vital power of a subtle kind that needs to be taken care of.

This energy is a force in man that is neither mental nor physical. It can't be reduced to either mind or matter nor "mindfulness" or "physicality."

However, this force is, indeed, often reduced in that way. Spiritual people say, "it is all in the mind." And materialists say, "the body is all there is."

We need to take the middle path between these two extremities to describe an important aspect of man and, indeed, of nature too.

We need to take the middle path, seeking a force that is neither matter nor mind.

So, what is this force?

It is *vril*. Also known as *od, ka chi,* and *prāṇa*.

Vril is mental energy, vital power. According to Albert Pike (see Chapter 10), it is the *Prima Materia* of alchemy. According to Bulwer-Lytton (ibid), Vril is *atmospheric magnetism, electrobiology, odic force.* In the terminology of Tice (see Chapter 9), vril is "universal fluid," prāṇa, vital force, nerve force, vital inner power, inner energy."

According to tradition, vril is the *Quinta Essentia*, the Philosopher's Stone, and the Fountain of Youth.

Quinta Essentia is the fifth element beyond earth, water, fire, and air.

It is equal to Prima Materia, elementary matter. In alchemical terms, it is *the Prima Materia of the Magnum Opus.*

It is the body of the Holy Spirit, the universal Agent, the Serpent devouring his own tail (Pike).

It is the Ether, nowadays formally denied by scientists, and is only known as a "gravity field," "action-at-a-distance," and other fanciful terms.

It is the Elixir of Life, the Fountain of Youth, the Philosopher's Stone...

Corresponding to the human realm, *Quinta Essentia* and all its synonyms are equal to vital power, mental energy, od, ka, vril. Vril is etherically present everywhere, both in nature and in man proper – because "wherever *anything* is, *Vril* is" (Tice).

Vril is the "Force" of Star Wars fame, an all-pervading power. As Yoda said:

> My ally is the Force, and a powerful ally it is. Life creates it, makes it grow. Its energy surrounds us and binds us. ... You must feel the Force around you; here, between you, me, the tree, the rock, everywhere, yes. ... A Jedi's strength flows from the Force. But beware of the dark side. Anger, fear, aggression; the dark side of the Force are they. Easily they flow, quick to join you in a fight. If once you start down the dark path, forever will it dominate your destiny, consume you it will.

The quintessence is this and more besides.

It is the "white stone written with a new name" mentioned in Revelations.

It is the Food of the Gods, *manna, ambrosia, soma*, Holy Water to my lips...

It is the Golden Tear from the Eye of Horus.

It is *the Astral Light* in Theosophical terminology.

It is dark energy, dark matter, and scalar energy (q.v. Chapter 14), zero point energy (q.v. Chapter 12). Nikola Tesla (1856-1943) said: "Electric energy is everywhere present in unlimited quantities and can drive the world's machinery without the need for coal, oil or gas."

Prima Materia (quintessence, Elixir of Life, vril, zero point energy etc.) is part of *the immanence field,* as we call it. It is part of *the Source*

Field that Wilcock speaks about (*The Source Field Investigations,* 2011).

The Black Sun of Agartha is made of this quintessence. And the Holy Grail is an artifact made of *Prima Materia*. And the rainbow in the sky.

In a Swedish context, we have the poet Bertel Gripenberg singing about "Den hemliga glöden" (the secret glow) that he worshipped, the flame of inspiration dwelling within. That is – vril.

Further, "*The Flame of Life*" was the English title of D'Annunzio's novel *Il fuoco* (1900), and this is in the same region, an artistic hymn to vitality, inspiration, and mental energy. This novel was explored in *Actionism* (2017).

Moreover, the element of *vafur,* mentioned by Viktor Rydberg in *Our Father's Godsaga,* could be vril. Vafur is an ancient Nordic term for elemental energy discharged in lightning.

Then we have the *Alpha-and-Omega* concept of Swedish author Dénis Lindbohm, stressing both the good and bad side of the vital force, as we saw with Star Wars. This is also clearly vril–related.

Summa summarum: Prima Materia is prevalent both in man and nature. It is both in the organic and the inorganic realm. You have it in you. In the form of vril. Because, where *anything* is, vril is.

This energy may be equal to the "omnium" that Flann O'Brien spoke about in a novel (see Chapter 14). "Omnium" implies "all" – and vril is an energy that is in all and everything, an all-pervading, unifying field of energy, an "electric, sparking power" flowing around you and inside of you.

So, say to yourself: *I have the power...!*

9. PAUL TICE

A s the reader knows by now, vril is an all-pervading *something*.

However, some repetition is always useful.

Vril is mental energy, vital power. According to Albert Pike, it is the *Prima Materia* of alchemy. And according to Bulwer-Lytton, vril is electrobiology and odic force (more on odic power in Chapter 11). And in the terminology of Tice, the focus of this chapter, vril is "universal fluid," prāṇa, vital force, nerve force, vital inner power, and inner energy.

In other words, this chapter looks at *Vril or Vital Magnetism* by Paul Tice (Chicago: McClurg & Co., 1911).

As you can see, Tice equals vril to "Vital Magnetism." For the record, he also calls it "vital-energy," "life-energy," and "life-force" [p. 7] Vril, a supposed Atlantean word meaning *life* [ibid], has the same root as Skt. *vṛdh* (grow, elevate, inspire). See also Latin *vir* (man, real man, soldier) and *virilis* (manly, manpower.); the Greek *vero* (hero); the Sanskrit *vira (hero, brave man)*, and the Anglo–Saxon *wer* (man) [p. 8].

Tice writes that:

Vril (…) is the inner power of action and movement of all material forms of the universe. [p. 15] That is, from atomic particles to living beings and beyond, Vril can be found in all matter. Vril (…) is the fine energy or force which enables material things to move of their own power – *the power within them.* [ibid; italics in original] Vril *energizes and moves* the physical structure, but does not *cause* it. [p. 21]

Vril is even beyond living beings. It is the force behind gravitation. Vril "pervades all space – it is immanent in the universal ether. Wherever *anything* is, *Vril* is". [p. 16]

Therefore, *will* is the director of the organism, the operator of it. *Vril* is the working power, that which visibly makes the organism go. However, vril is more of a mental power than a physical force – or a kind of mix of both.

Vril is indeed a subtle thing, something in between mind and matter. It is *psycho-physical* rather than merely physical or psychic. The concept of "*élan vital*" by Bergson captures the essence of vril.

Mind, Vril, and Matter are the three basic principles of reality, dependent upon each other for their activities. It is *the triangle of being,* as Tice says.

Vril explains a lot of psychic phenomena, since Vril permeates everything, both matter, and mind. It is *immanent in thought processes,* but it is not identical to the mind. [p. 10] All matter has vril, that is, life, in it; it is the idea of *hylozoism,* "life in matter" by Henry T. Laurency.

The mind isn't just thought. Instead, the mind is *the original cause* of thought. "Thought [...] is a manifestation of mind, assisted by Vril." [p. 23], and vril is active in every thought process.

The mind can produce effects from a distance with the power of vril, as Tice says. This is similar to a phenomenon in physics called "action at a distance." It is explained by the invisible presence of vril.

Mentalism (to project your mental power, e.g., hypnosis), then, is vril in action. Thus, I hold, vril explains more than merely saying, "it is all in the mind."

A thought cannot be generated or projected without vril. [p. 25-26]

You can energize your thought with vril. [p. 26]

Since vril energy can't be destroyed, it is merely transformed from one state to another. We use it willfully but don't create it.

> Vril ... is the fine energy or force which enables material things to move of their own power – *the power within them.* [p. 15]

Vril is the élan vital, survival instinct, animalistic drive, similar to *od, ka, chi,* and the *Force* of Star Wars. It is the force that transforms the seed into a tree, an embryo into a man (more on vril affecting embryonic biology in Chapter 12).

Vril energy performs the work, directed by will-thought.

Vril is "morally neutral" and can be used for good and evil purposes. When used with good intentions, it creates beneficial results.

Vril is consumed by emotion, by unrestrained *feeling*. Contrariwise, soberly employed will-thought and will-directed *thinking* don't spend much vril. If the thought is positive, it might even replenish vril. This, again, underlines the need for good intent when employing vril.

According to Tice, vril is stored in the nervous system of the human organism.

The organism resupplies vril with food, water, and – to a rather high degree – air.

However, vril is replenished by the power of will-thought, through "mental alchemy," which entails imagining what you want and manifesting it via will. It is achieved by creating strong, positive mental images and projecting them into the outer world with willpower. *Willpower and vision* are the keywords.

Imagine vril as present in the atmosphere, acting as a tangible energy current or electric presence. Next, imagine the nervous system absorbing vril by force of will. Finally, command the system to absorb a greater amount of vril.

Form a mental image of this, anchor it in the subconscious mind, then reinforce and enforce it by the will; thus, you gain an increased power of absorption of vril.

Will the vril absorption and feel that it is underway.

The absorption of vril is dependent on will-thought. The application of will-thought entails the wisdom of esoteric theory, and its coda, according to Tice, is: "The secret of mental alchemy may be stated as consisting first, last and always, of the art of mental imagining, reinforced by the will." In other words: willpower and vision...!

"Mental alchemy creates inspiring images and projects them into the world with willpower." [p. 90] When using this process, physical exertion should be minimal, and jerky, ugly motions should be avoided. It requires poise for quiet execution and the need for rest when sitting and lying down; all this is paramount to the adept. On a more cautious note,

> Triflers who enter the field of psychism or occultism frequently are brought to a rather vigorous realization of the fact that they are but pygmies playing with titanic forces. [p. 105]

Furthermore, the psychic aspect of vril is paramount:

> Vril is the real *force* or *energy* in all manifestations of thought-force – the mind merely serving to project that force by the will, and to color it by the idea or feeling held in the mind. The thought sent forth is colored and charged with Vril by the strength of the feeling or desire manifested, in the majority of cases. [p. 118]

Now that we have explored the work of Tice, it is time to examine Edouard Schuré's *The Great Initiates* (London: William Rider & Sons, 1920). This book doesn't mention vril *per se*. However, Schuré is definitely in the vril zone (by mentioning *odyl*, which is close enough).

Drawing inspiration from Schuré, it is reasonable to deduce that vril is a *subtle fluid* and a *universal fluid*. It is astral light, astral energy; it is the substance of the astral body. Thus, affirming the existence of vril is one of many ways of letting us *consciously connect with the astral*. Regarding terminology, it is also clear that vril is "the Solar Word" of mysticism and the World Soul of Plotinus, the all-pervading entity by some called Cybele-Maïa: "the veil of Isis, the mantle of Cybele" (Schuré). Thus: vril is od, odil, odyl (Reichenbach, q.v. Chapter 11), the Force, chi, ka, prāṇa, and maybe even Kundalini. Vril is the World Soul embracing all and in sympathy with all, even the soul of the individual.

10. VARIOUS VRIL GURUS

I will now look at various figures having spoken about this "vital power." Bulwer–Lytton explicitly called this vril, and others are referring to the same phenomenon.

Firstly, I will quote some lines from Albert Pike (1809–1891). He knew of this and the powers of the human individual regarding the immanent power around us and inside us.

Below we find an excerpt from Pike's treatise *Morals and Dogma* (1871). He speaks of will and the power associated with it. The power of will is similar to "human magnetism" (od, ka, chi, prāṇa, vril); vocabulary aside, this is attested by Pike. The below excerpt transcends both science and religion; it elevates human power into more than mere vitality *and* more than mere *influxus* of spirit.

I intimated the same in Chapter 8. In explaining the human condition, there is more than the mind *and* more than physicality. Pike knew this.

For instance, he emphasized the existence of will; very few philosophers do. But Pike said:

> [M]an knows but little of the powers of the human will, and imperfectly appreciates them; since he knows nothing as to the nature of the will and its mode of operation. He concludes: "... a concentrated effort of the will is in every case necessary to success."

Following this Pike points to the heart of the matter, speaking of a "most potent force"; the quote stands for itself:

> There is in nature one most potent force, by means whereof a single man, who could possess himself of it, and should know how to direct it, could revolutionize and change the face of the world.

He continues to say that this force was known to the ancients – he doesn't mention *od, ka, chi, prāṇa, or vril,* but this is what he refers to.

> This force was known to the ancients. It is a universal agent whose Supreme law is equilibrium, and whereby, if science can but learn how to control it, it will be possible to change the order of the Seasons, to produce in the night the phenomena of day, to send a thought in an instant round the world, to heal or slay at a distance, to give our words universal success, and make them reverberate everywhere.

Furthermore:

This agent, partially revealed by the blind guesses of the disciples of Mesmer, is precisely what the Adepts of the middle ages called *the elementary matter of the great work* [Prima Materia of the Magnum Opus]. The Gnostics held that it composed the igneous body of the Holy Spirit; and it was adored in the secret rites of the Sabbat or the Temple, under the hieroglyphic figure of Baphomet or the hermaphroditic goat of Mendes.

There is a Life-Principle of the world, a universal agent, wherein are two natures and a double current, of love and wrath. This ambient fluid penetrates everything. It is a ray detached from the glory of the Sun, and fixed by the weight of the atmosphere and the central attraction. It is the body of the Holy Spirit, the universal Agent, the Serpent devouring his own tail. With this electro-magnetic ether, this vital and luminous caloric, the ancients and the alchemists were familiar. Of this agent, that phase of modern ignorance termed physical science talks incoherently, knowing naught of it save its effects; and theology might apply to it all its pretended definitions of spirit. Quiescent, it is appreciable by no human sense; disturbed or in movement, none can explain its mode of action; and to term it a 'fluid,' and speak of its 'currents,' is but to veil a profound ignorance under a cloud of words.

Force attracts force, life attracts life, health attracts health. It is a law of nature." [Albert Pike, *Morals and Dogma*, 1871, p. 734–735]

Edward Bulwer-Lytton (1803–1873) also spoke of vril.

If you have heard of the popular literary phrase "It was a dark and stormy night," then you may also be aware that Bulwer-Lytton's novel *Paul Clifford* (1830) begins this way.

Bulwer-Lytton was a prolific British writer; he wrote novels such as *The Last Days of Pompeii* and *Rienzi, the Last of the Roman Tribunes.* Wagner based his famous opera on the latter.

More importantly, in 1871 Bulwer-Lytton wrote *Vril, the Power of the Coming Race.*

This novel is *symbolically* a major source of the concept of vril proper. Bulwer-Lytton's book probably brought mankind the first mention of the concept – the first expression of this eternal force in terms of vril.

However, the book is a novel. It is fiction. Still, what it says about vril is coherent and in line with the picture of "vital power" I am now attempting to paint.

Vril, the Power of the Coming Race, begins with the narrator climbing down a cave. After a while, he finds himself in a subterranean land lit by lamps. It seems to be a giant cave where the roof isn't discernible.

He meets people there who are noble and advanced. They have lights, they have robots serving them, and they have powerful weapons. The energy source for all this is said to be vril.

When trying to explain vril to us, the narrator places it in the region of *atmospheric magnetism, mesmerism, electrobiology,* and *odic force.* That is in harmony with what I wrote previously.

The people the narrator has met, the subterranean race, are called *Vril-ya.* With instruments called *vril conductors,* the Vril-ya "can exercise influence over minds" [p. 17]. The Vril-ya use telepathy with vril as a medium. As Paul Tice would say, *they energize thought with vril.* The vril conductor amplifies the power of the thought.

The function of this vril conductor isn't described by Bulwer-Lytton's narrator. Rather, he says that he himself has been hypnotized into learning the language of the Vril–ya: "... it was through the agency of vril, while I had been placed in the state of trance, that I had been made acquainted with the rudiments of their language" [ibid].

The vril conductor might, however, be equal or similar to (or be a component of) *the Vril staff,* another tool used by the Vril-ya. With good intent, it can cure. With hostile intent, it is a powerful weapon. "The fire lodged in the hollow of a rod directed by the hand of a child could shatter the strongest fortress, or cleave its burning way from the van to the rear of an embattled host." [p. 20]

Vril is mentioned throughout the novel, but mostly as an energy source. There is no further ambition to penetrate its secrets. Instead, the narrator concentrates on things like the language of the Vril-ya, its societal organization, and a love story between him and a Vril-ya woman.

Inside earth lives a superman race with powerful weapons. That's the gist of the novel. It is written in a stiff, pedantic style, but it is a novel to return to, a novel with a lot of mystery surrounding it. For example, how did Bulwer-Lytton get the idea for it? And, is it based on truth?

As we've seen, Nikola Tesla spoke about electricity abounding in the atmosphere: "Electric energy is everywhere present in unlimited quantities and can drive the world's machinery without the need for coal, oil or gas." Bulwer-Lytton is on the same track with his concept of "atmospheric magnetism," mentioned above as a synonym for vril. In other words, vril is all around us, in the air, as an invisible presence in the air.

This is evident when Bulwer-Lytton quotes the scientist Michael Faraday (1791-1867) in his novel.

When first presented with the concept of vril, the narrator says that he is stupefied. Nonetheless, he can liken it to magnetism and galvanism, and also like Faraday "intimates under the ... term of correlation" [p. 16]. He then quotes Faraday directly:

> I have long held an opinion, almost amounting to a conviction, in common, I believe, with many other lovers of natural knowledge, that the various forms under which the forces of matter are made manifest have one common origin; or, in other words, are so directly related and mutually dependent, that they are convertible, as it were, into one another, and

possess equivalents of power in their action. [Faraday after Bulwer-Lytton, ibid]

This captures it all very well. This intimates the all-pervading nature of vril: "where anything is, Vril is" (Tice), and the equality of vril with *quinta essentia*, *prima materia*, the ether, etc. It is omnipresent; it is *Omnium*...!

Bulwer-Lytton probably knew more about this than what he disclosed. He was a novelist and artist at heart, a weaver of tales with fictitious embroidery, and in *Vril or the Power of the Coming Race,* he depicted an etherically driven society in this way – the artistic way, the novelist way. It becomes a little unsystematic, but what he says is feasible for a student of human magnetism or of the vital power present in nature and in man.

However, we must ask: how much did he really know? About vril, and about subterranean supermen?

Certainly, Bulwer-Lytton knew more than what the novel may convey to us. For example, in 1842, he wrote the novel *Zanoni*. One element of this work was a mysterious brotherhood spiritually ruling the world, like the *mahatmas.* Blavatsky also spoke of this. This novel is especially important for followers of occultism because of "the suspicion – actively fostered by its author – that the work is not a fictional account of a mythical fraternity, but an accurate depiction of a real brotherhood of immortals" [French].

Bulwer-Lytton knew a lot, a lot more than what is revealed in his novels.

Finally, in this trilogy of vril gurus, we turn to Thoth.

The Emerald Tablets of Thoth is a book. It is written by Thoth, who is equivalent to the Greek God Hermes. It is a book of wisdom told by this man-god who was born in Atlantis, founded the Egyptian culture, and traveled astrally in space.

In this examination, I will focus on the points Thoth provides concerning vril, od, ka, chi. He doesn't mention these terms, but he does mention "life, energy, and ether."

In *Tablet One: Thoth the Atlantean* Thoth says that in the Halls of Amenti, "the river of life flows eternally onward." Sojourning there invigorates him; when leaving, he has his "strength and power renewed."

Speaking of his Atlantean days, he writes, "strong were we with the power drawn from the eternal fire…"

After the fall of Atlantis, Thoth went to Egypt to start civilization anew. Landing there in this land of *Khem,* he met hairy barbarians who attacked him and his crew. But Thoth merely raised his staff "and directed a ray of vibration, striking them in their tracks as fragments of stone of the mountain." In other words, he killed them with a vril weapon, driven by willpower and vision.

He then built the pyramid of Giza, "using the power that overcomes Earth force." At the apex, he set a crystal, "sending the ray into the 'Time-Space,' drawing the force from out of the ether." This force, of course, is vril power.

I suspect that Thoth built the pyramid using willpower and vision, employing vril. Which, by the way, is the way anything is built; the crucial difference is that for ordinary men, the process is slower.

In *Tablet Four: The Space Born,* he speaks of his astral journeys. One planet, in particular, was special:

> Some I found who had conquered the ether.
> Free of space were they while yet they were men.
> Using the force that is the foundation of ALL things [vril],
> far in space constructed they a planet,
> drawn by the force that flows through the ALL;
> condensing, coalescing the ether into forms,
> that grew as they willed.

In other words, this is about willpower and vision shaping the ether into anything you wish.

Thoth *saw them create gigantic cities of rose and gold from out of the ether,* forming in their mind a picture that took shape and grew into material reality.

The Dweller built his temple in Atlantis in the same way (*Tablet Five, The Dweller of Unal*). After building it, he filled it with etherical forms that became real: "Builded HE then, within it, great chambers, // filled them with forms called forth from the ETHER, // filled them with wisdom called forth by His mind."

Furthermore: the stars stay in their courses due to "by primordial mist," which is the vril.

Man is tripartite *à la* physical, astral, and mental = body, vril, and mind (*Tablet Fifteen, The Secret of Secrets*). This is the same pattern provided by Paul Tice.

11. ODIC POWER

Vril energy has many synonyms. One of them is *od* or *odic power*. For instance, Bulwer-Lytton mentioned "odic force" as something akin to Vril.

It was the German Scholar Baron Carl von Reichenbach (1788-1869) who conceptualized the vital energy of man as the odic force, odyl or od. It is the same as the Egyptian ka, the Hindu prāṇa, and the Taoist chi, though in a West European style.

In other words, odic force is vril, vril is od...

Odic force can be seen as *intuition, inspiration, inebriation.* I spoke of this in Actionism (2017) as "movement as a state."

This is what we come to think about today regarding od, "action as being," living, and Actionist vitalism.

It is about Od-Svipdag fighting his way to the underworld and returning to Freya in Asgard. As such, this is one of many representations of the "vīra-valkyrie pattern." Also, most fittingly, the Icelandic word "*odr*" means "divine madness, frantic, furious, vehement, eager" – and "mind, feeling" and "song, poetry." It is certainly a concept for "astral war as astral art" and for "the spirit of song is war" as Södergran said.

This is the astral fight as "inspiration and inebriation" of combat trance, spurred on by an image of the beloved, as was the driving force of Od–Svipdag.

Od was Freya's husband, mentioned in the Edda as a man who left her and then never returned. However, in *Our Fathers' Godsaga*, Viktor Rydberg connected Od with another Edda figure, the elf Svipdag, who in the narrative poem "Grougaldr" travels through the underworld – and, in "Fjölsvinnsmal," reunites with the Goddess of Love in Asgard–Agartha's sublime pastures.

Interestingly, od has been connected to the chief Asa god, Odin. Odin is the god of "war, poetry, and ecstasy," of shamanic song and the din of battle. Odin personifies the odic force.

As such, as in any example of human magnetism, the odic force can be both negative and positive, fruitful as well as damaging. One must rein it in and take responsibility for its power, a power all human beings have within. Use it wrongly and be damned; use it properly and be a divine, a *Sonnenmensch vīra*.

The odic force is real, Odin is real, and Od–Svipdag searching for Freya is real. Inspiration, inebriation, initiation; all in one and one in all.

12. ZERO POINT ENERGY

Previously, I quoted Nikola Tesla: "Electric energy is everywhere present in unlimited quantities and can drive the world's machinery without the need for coal, oil or gas."

This is a fine summation of *zero point energy* and what I mentioned earlier. Moreover, zero point field research is still studied today.

In the book *The Field – The Quest for the Secret Force of the Universe,* written by Lynne McTaggart and originally published in 2001, we find vril territory. McTaggart doesn't explicitly utilize that term, but she mentions *chi* (spelling it *qi*).

So what is the zero point? McTaggart explains it, and we summarize her thoughts below.

In the early 20th century, quantum mechanics realized that the universe is not static. It is a cauldron of subatomic particles emerging and disappearing in a constant process. The very fabric of reality seemed to be a field of energy constantly interacting with all subatomic matter. The foundation of the universe was a vast quantum field.

This quality of constant subatomic movement was discovered by German physicist Werner

Heisenberg (1901-1976). He showed that you couldn't determine both the energy and the direction of a particle; this is also known as *the uncertainty principle.* Any given, brief subatomic event includes a lot of unknown energy; it is infinitely small and infinitely energetic...!

The particles created in these brief encounters are called *virtual particles,* only existing while the energy exchange takes place, the time of uncertainty intimated by the uncertainty principle.

This subatomic dance takes place in the zero point field. It was given the value of *zero* because movement in this field can still be measured at absolute zero temperature, at minus 273 Celsius, a state of energy where no movement should appear. Zero point energy was the energy that was left in the maximum vacuum at the lowest possible temperature, as close to zero as possible in a subatomic movement.

Due to the uncertainty principle, some residual oscillations will always remain, depending on the exchange between the virtual particles. However, scientists have always disregarded this because it was always there. They ignored it, seeing it as an insignificant anomaly.

Nevertheless, scientist Timothy Boyer (1941-) meant that the energy flow of the zero point field could explain many anomalies of quantum mechanics. With the zero point field, one could actually clarify the quantum world with classic Newtonian physics. Hal Puthoff (1936-) also speculated about using the zero point field as an energy source.

Quantum mechanics shows us that we live in a sea of movement, a quantum sea of light. Earlier in the 19th century Michael Faraday intimated another field, the *electromagnetic field.* All such fields connect to the zero point field; it is a field of fields. A lot of energy is there, in any part of it, in any particle. Physicist Richard Feynman said that the energy of one cubic meter of space is enough to boil the water of all the seas on earth.

The zero point field told the more open-minded scientists (like Hal Puthoff) that all the matter in the universe was connected by waves. These waves were like the Chinese concept of *chi* – an all-pervading energy field. It was like the Biblical "let there be light," a light from which we then saw the emanation of solid matter, such as the earth.

What Hal Puthoff meant (in a paper to Physical Review) was that the stability of matter depends on this dynamic exchange of subatomic particles in the zero point field. All the time, electrons lose and gain energy from the zero point field in a dynamic balance giving all matter its stability.

That is, matter is seemingly stable, but its core quality is a flow of particles in the zero point field. *Panta rei:* all is change, all is flow, and with *will,* we can take command of this flow. This is about the power of mind over matter; we create our world. McTaggart touches on this in her book. For example, Action-at-a-distance, non-locality, ESP, levitation, clairvoyance, precognition, spiritual healing, and the collective unconscious could all be explained by their share in the zero point field. For instance, the clairvoyant gets his visions by looking into the zero point field.

Biophotons, subatomic particles making us alive, have their source in zero point field occurrences. The cell communicates with biophotons; this can explain both the development from a single-cell embryo into an organism (an animal, a man, etc.) and the "orchestration of cellular processes." Biophotonic emissions can explain both morphogenetics and the coordination and communication between cells. And all these, of course, are things that modern science can't explain.

Memory, inspiration, dreams; these and other mental mysteries can be explained by connecting them to the zero point field. We dream, create, and remember by tapping into the zero point field.

Even visual sight, the everyday perception of everyday objects, can be explained with reference to the zero point. We don't see the objects as such, we see their quantum information, and from this, we construct our image of the world. Thus, to perceive the world would be equal to tuning into the zero point field.

The zero point field is the ultimate storage medium. It is the way to access the past and the future, and a synonym for *time-space* – that is, the metaphysical realm where we can surpass everyday movement in space and also move in time. A timeless sphere devoid of separation – the astral world –this is the zero point field.

That would support another idea suggested by McTaggart: when we die, we return to the zero point field. Thus, when we die, we return to the astral...! McTaggart bestows old-school metaphysics with a new tinge, a quantum physical tinge.

The zero point field is also what orthodox science calls "the vacuum." However, this vacuum isn't empty. As Aldous Huxley said, *space is alive with waves and particles, a gigantic and cosmic jazz..!*

Science fiction author Arthur C. Clarke touches on the same thing in his novel *3001,* referring to Puthoff and saying that empty space is a cauldron of boiling energies (the zero point field). Inertia and gravity are electromagnetic phenomena occurring because of interaction with that field. Every force is there; Faraday once tried to link gravity to magnetism, but he couldn't prove it. Now, however, with the theories of Puthoff and others, inertia and gravity could be conceptually linked and overcome. This leads to space; we could have an energy-free space drive, an anti-gravity engine. We could have craft traveling at thousands of km/h.

The zero point perspective touches on a lot of metaphysical concepts beyond mere atmospheric electricity. McTaggart briefly mentions such luminaries as David Bohm and Rupert Sheldrake; however, I won't discuss them in this book because I have already covered them in *Borderline* (2016).

McTaggart says that "the centre holds, and we are holding it"... The universe needs a spectator; *die Welt als Wille und Vorstellung.* As we are, so we see. We are co-creators of the world with God.

In a more narrow sense, McTaggart's coda is: communication is subatomic. An invisible field, permeating and supporting the universe, stores all kinds of information and enables all forms of communication.

The zero point perspective enables a Newtonian explanation of quantum physics (Boyer, Puthoff). Thus, from a *school-scientific* point of view, we could get a unified description of the world using classic physics without having to resort to a specialized quantum physical description of supposedly weird phenomena – phenomena like "things at one time existing and not existing at another" (the uncertainty principle), or "things spookily affecting each other at a distance" (action-at-a-distance). By acknowledging the zero point field, we can scientifically explain almost anything in the physical universe regarding the movement of planets, earthly objects, and of atoms and subatomic particles.

Knowledge of the zero point connects with the premise of this book because Vril, the quintessence, omnium etc. is invisible. It is a force, a field, a subatomic occurrence. With McTaggart's theory, summarized above, we now have a scientific explanation to it, a quantum physical background to it, for anyone who requires this background.

In other words, there is a quantum connection between the earth, living beings, and the zero point field. We are striving toward a unified concept of the universe, a concept of everything, of Omnium. This concept would reconcile mind with matter, art with science, and science with religion.

The zero point field is a land of subatomic vibrations, present everywhere: in space, on earth, and in ourselves. According to McTaggart, zero point energy exists in a system of fields exchanging energy, linking everything and all, being present in both mind and matter, in bodies as well as in solid matter.

The all-pervading life force – vril, chi, prana – can be described as the zero point field, a living energy field that not even scientists can deny. This all-encompassing energy field will never go away; it resonates with everything.

McTaggart's book has been reviewed and has several quality reviews. Here is an inspirational quote from one that explores the subject from both a scientific and a traditional viewpoint, stating that the zero point field is akin to the Biblical concept of *manna*.

> This is the most exciting thing I can think of; the discovery of a substance that is half way between spirit and matter! A substance that can improve the food we eat and our health from that food at the same time! A substance that ties into the most fundamental discoveries of modern science! A substance that was known to ancient mystics and alchemists! A substance that accesses the zero point for technology like energy production and levitation! Is there anything more full of wonder than this?[1]

---

[1] http://www.subtleenergies.com/ormus/tw/review.htm

I am quantum non–locality...

I am everywhere – and nowhere. I am all beings – and none.

Call me – Vril power Superman. I will give mankind the stars.

13. SUPERMAN MUSINGS

I n this chapter, I will look at the concept of the superman. The overman. The next step in the evolution of man: "Man is a rope stretched between animal and superman." The superman is the embodiment of vril power.

The angle we will examine here is that of Nietzsche and selected Science Fiction authors. From a non–mystical starting point, they all captured some vital aspects of the superman condition. The theme of this chapter is a "phenomenological" overview of supermanism, a sketch of the land of *superomismo* as Nietzsche and others conceived of it, intending to show how a "vril-powered life" could look.

1.

Nietzsche coined the very term "superman." In *Thus Spake Zarathustra,* he says that man is something to be overcome; man shall strive to be more than he is. He shall elevate himself into a virtual godhead and become a dancing Dionysos, a man possessed by Odin.

Nietzsche intimated the presence of Odin in the poem "To the Unknown God" from 1863-64. And I covered the spiritual side of *Thus Spake Zarathustra* in both *Borderline* and *Actionism.*

In a letter to a friend (Meta von Salis), Nietzsche wrote:

> Fraulein von Salis. The world is transfigured, for God is on the earth. Do not you see how all the heavens rejoice?

This was written shortly before his mental collapse. But these lines are perfectly salient. If a god walks the earth, it would indeed be transfigured, and the heavens would rejoice. Nietzsche's letter illustrates the state of a "god incarnated as a man." Even the madness could be seen as immanently divine.

However, the Übermensch concept wasn't purely divine elevation and Dionysian ecstasy. His work implies human perfection. Figures such as Goethe, Montaigne, Voltaire, and Napoleon were good examples of this. They fulfilled the dictum, "be all that you can be."

So, all you superman aspirants out there, becoming supermen isn't very hard. Just perfect your talents and shine.

We mentioned "transfiguration" earlier.

In *The Will to Power*, Nietzsche explains divine supermanism in nuce: "[M]an becomes the transfigurer of existence when he learns to transfigure himself." [Nietzsche, *The Will to Power*, p. 434]

Moreover, in the same book, we find this extremely apt citation:

> If we affirm one single moment, we thus affirm not only ourselves but all existence. For nothing is self-sufficient, neither in us ourselves nor in things; and if our soul has trembled with happiness and sounded like a harp string just once, all eternity was needed to produce this one event—and in this single moment of affirmation all eternity was called good, redeemed, justified, and affirmed. [ibid, p. 532–533]

Furthermore, here are two quotes from *Will to* Power concerning individual strength.

> 1. I teach the No to all that makes weak—that exhausts. I teach the Yes to all that strengthens, that stores up strength, that justifies the feeling of strength. [p. 33]

> 2. It is only a question of strength: to have all the morbid traits of the century, but to balance them through a superabundant, recuperative strength. The strong man. [p. 524]

Nietzsche, therefore, is the superman abounding in vril, in all but name. This is profoundly manifested through his alter ego Zarathustra in *Thus Spake Zarathustra*. The last lines of the book should suffice to illustrate the power exuding from it in its best parts, the vital energy virtually dripping off the page:

> Do I then strive after *happiness?* I strive after my *work!* ... This is *my* morning, *my* day beginneth: *arise now, arise, thou great noontide!"* Thus spake Zarathustra and left his cave, glowing and strong, like a morning sun coming out of gloomy mountains. [p. 368, Thomas Common translation]

2.

Are there more superpowers and more vital energy to be revealed through literature...? One fine effort to capture the nature of supermanism is evident in the works of Robert A. Heinlein. He may not have had the same stylistic flair, but he does strive to show us, symbolically and formally, what defines a genius, and what might be seen as a kind of superman.

Heinlein doesn't speak of vital power, nor does he speak of will, that necessary part of the superman parcel, but he gets a lot of other points correct. The prime explain of this is contained in the novelette "Gulf." I spoke of this in by book *Science Fiction Seen From the Right:*

> *Gulf* gives us *in nuce* the Heinlein creed of rationalism, otherwise evangelized in *Stranger In a Strange Land* and implicitly in almost every Heinlein story. The ideal is to be a studied man, to take your Ph.D., to learn and use your mental faculties to the utmost. To destroy all the lies devised in the past and shed light over all the darkness...! [Svensson 2016, p. 26]

Regarding the superman aspect of "Gulf," one aspect of this is *speedtalk.* The argument is that ordinary talk contains a lot of superfluous words, so instead, we should talk in short formulas, in reduced groups of sounds containing way much more info than ordinary sentences of words. In other words, if we did away with the linguistic chaff, we could convey so much more information. However, I don't see this as a viable alternative, since *language isn't logical; it is sociological...* Speedtalk might be a kind of *volapuk* or *esperanto*, a logical language looking good in theory but is emotionally hard to speak fluently by a sentient being.

In the story, we only get snippets of this talk, thankfully, because it is unspeakable, which goes to show that getting rid of unnecessary information and unnecessary words is a misconceived enterprise.

However, Heinlein's way of depicting speedtalk has a symbolic quality; it represents the will to change the way we ordinarily do things.

Heinlein doesn't use the word "will" in his superman portrait, but it is implicit in his work. For example, a man constantly intent on becoming smarter and better at thinking is a will-driven person. Will-and-thought in harmony is a strong force. Willpower and vision...!

3.

Heinlein never referred to Nietzsche, however. This is also typical of several Science Fiction writers, the mainstay of European and American writers of *fantastika* from Verne and on.

The basis for this claim is the Science Fiction Encyclopedia. In it, we have the entry "superman."[2] For instance, it says that no visible influence from Nietzsche can be found in Science Fiction literature. However, the Science Fiction superman and the Nietzschean superman are kind of similar. They are atheists; they are unmystical, seemingly unrelated to the Western spiritual tradition.

Nietzsche, for one, wrote of concepts such as "the will to power" and "eternal recurrence" as incentives for raising yourself above everyday man, but does he really teach us "how to do it"...? Sometimes he does but in a vague manner.

We also have Heinlein's portrait of the *genial* condition, the superman as a super-intellect.

Of course, there are more colorful, "fairy-tale" Science Fiction supermen. Often, they just happen to be more powerful than the average human. They are heroic but mindless. The prime example of a Science Fiction superman who is just "super" would be the comic book hero Superman; he is an alien on Earth who discovers that his natural talents on Earth become super talents – like being able to fly and having abnormal strength.

The DC Comics Superman never has to summon up his willpower, absorb vril, or meditate in order to become super strong. He is simply super

---

[2]   [http://www.sf–encyclopedia.com/entry/superman].

strong by nature. The DC Superman is a comic book figure, a graphic phenomenon.

However, we also have Science Fiction literature proper, the textual, more epic art form. Here we also find a superman with alien heritage: Gil Gosseyn of van Vogt's *The World of Null-A* (1945). For instance, he has two brains, but that isn't very scientific; just a fairy tale in Science Fiction, but it is a treasure trove of myth and metaphor. However, for this discussion, Gil Gosseyn hasn't much to offer. He just *is* a superman with super talents, there to use when the plot demands it.

These alluring hints of the superman condition occur in the novel. For example, a lie detector delivers the following verdict on Gil Gosseyn: "There is an aura of unique strength about him." [p. 25]

Then there is "the Null-A training" the hero has undergone. Null-A equals "non-Aristotelean," which, in this context, means anti-reductionist and holistic. This is the program; you must avoid reductionism, you must be holistic...! That's the Null-A training. van Vogt only explains this vaguely; nevertheless, "Null-A" is a fascinating concept in the realm of the spiritual, holistic outlook Actionism favors. The holistic pattern is there, and it can be a container for the whole spiritual circus we direct.

Gil Gosseyn is a heroic figure who performs amazing feats. Mostly his method isn't explained, which could place him in the "mindless hero" category along with Superman, James Bond, and all the rest. van Vogt had a predilection for holistic heroes in other works too, such as Eliot Grosvenor in *The Voyage of the Space Beagle* (1950). Grosvenor is a *nexialist,* there to solve problems that the more narrow minded professionals of the crew can't see. This, too, intimates holism.

Even more topical is van Vogt's novel *Slan* (1946). The young hero is evolving into a superman – slowly – because becoming one takes time to realize. This is a rather credible angle to supermanism. Otherwise, *Slan* gives us the usual "marvels upon marvels" of the Science Fiction story, of Faustian fantastika; the hero is heroic because he is the hero. No descriptions are provided to understand the superhuman condition. There is no real process of education, of ascending the learning curve.

4.

Concerning mindless heroes, the grey-area figures of energetic supermanism; one example is Donal Graeme of Gordon R. Dickson's *Dorsai!* novel (1960). As part of a culture of mercenaries, Graeme becomes a super-soldier, changing the face of the interstellar culture he lives in. He faces problems and solves them, just like that. He is a bit like a facetious Asimov-type of hero; he just knows how to do it. Despite the superficially transparent, "modern science" attitude of the text, the whims and unexplained intuitions do make the plot work. In the end, Graeme leaps and soars, literally, into vril-power territory. However, there is no explanation for this; he just does it. So Graeme is heroic but mindless, but with an alluring nature.

You could read spirit into everything you see. Any sufficiently heroic text can be a discreet vril document, if you set your mind to it. In the genre of Science Fiction, we find early space opera heroes like Curt Nelson, John Ulnar, and Kim Kinnison could be vril-endowed heroes, but it's mostly in the eye of the beholder.

Concerning vril proper, there is a Science Fiction story on this, Heinlein's novella *Waldo* (1950). It begins as a tale of atomic power running the world; power is radiated everywhere to fuel cars and power homes. Then, one day, the system fails. A hex doctor examines the problem, and then the machines work again – now driven by "magic" (that's the term used), that is, immanent electricity, zero point energy, vril. "Magic is loose in the world!" is the byword. And vril is akin to magic.

The hex doctor says that there is power everywhere, which is reminiscent of the Tesla quote I have reproduced many times in this book: "Electric energy is everywhere present in unlimited quantities and can drive the world's machinery without the need for coal, oil or gas."

In *Waldo,* this becomes the new power source. The machines don't run on harmful radiated power generated by even more harmful nuclear fission. They run on magic, Heinlein says; on vril, *I* say. However, they are the same – for example, in Heinlein's story, the hex doctor speaks of *having to believe* in this power to make it work; truly, a vril-related truth...! For, as Tice told us in Chapter 9, absorbing vril depends on willpower and vision,

Heinlein could pull spiritual aces like this out of his sleeve; sometimes Dickson and Asimov also hint that *Western Modern Science*™ doesn't have all the answers. *Waldo* is a fine example of grey area Science Fiction, depicting a modern world run by free energy – zero point energy – vril.

5.

There is a landmark Science Fiction *film* that refers to Nietzsche: Stanley Kubrick's *2001, A Space Odyssey* (1968). The opening credits feature the intro to Richard Strauss's *Also Sprach Zarathustra*, a musical piece about Nietzsche's fictitious preacher who declared the superman. This connects to the film's plot because primordial man developed from a near-animal to a tool-using master of nature, a semi-intelligent being. With time this leads to the modern man who eventually becomes a space-faring species.

In the space age, a mystic signal from the moon urges mankind to go to the surroundings of Saturn to examine a strange artifact. Once near it, the man doing the research is drawn into it and is taken to a parallel universe. At the end of this trip, mysterious aliens, which we don't get to see, raise him to another level of development.

He has become a Starchild, soon to grow into a superman and take over the world. This is what the plot reveals to Nietzschean music...! So, the connection between Nietzsche and Science Fiction does exist. On the formal level, it is only to be found in the film; the Nietzsche symphonic was included thanks to the director, Stanely Kubrick, and not the scriptwriter, Science Fiction author Arthur C. Clarke.

Clarke envisioned the scenario and its main development. He later wrote a novel based on the script. Again, the novel *2001* has no mention of Nietzsche; however, it does have some indications of how to become superman, and of how the astronaut-turned Starchild becomes the next stage in human history. The spaceman goes from human to god-like status in a captivating saga. First, the alien intelligence urges him to explore his life and overcome any mental hurdles still lingering, just as any yoga, magic, or shamanistic adept must do. He then becomes *clear;* he becomes C3 in Actionist lingo: Calm, Cool, and Collected. He has left his ordinary human self behind, and he is now ready for rebirth – as a Starchild, a man of the future.

For a Science Fiction story, this is well described. In the film, the process is a little abrupt with the step from man to Starchild. Overall, however, approaching *2001*, the book and film, as a single work, is alluring in the same way that van Vogt and others are alluring with their allusions to supermanism. The film's use of the *Also Sprach Zarathustra* theme consummates the union, the marriage of Nietzschean *supermanism* to Science Fiction *supermanism.*

14. HUMAN MAGNETISM MARGINALIA

In the previous chapters, I mentioned *omnium*. This was a magical substance discovered by author Flann O'Brien.

In his novel *The Third Policeman* (1967), we read of omnium, an energy which, by various wavelengths, expresses everything in the universe: light, sound, and solid matter. Those in the know can harness omnium from one source and convert it into another, like capturing a sound and using it to light a room.

Concentrated omnium can be used to manifest anything.

In other words: omnium is a fantastic thing, capturing the magic of vril, od, and zero point energy.

One of the many labels for omnium, vril, the quintessence, etc., is *prima materia*. One reference to this provides good descriptions of it, though it is spelled throughout as "prima matra." Prima materia is the traditional spelling.

The author, Johannine Grove, says that prima materia

> ... is an ancient alchemical term that means prime unviolated first matter, and covers any form of matter that is resonant with the original first matter. [...]

And continues on to state that

> According to Tehuti / Thoth, originally this planet was entirely a spiritual creation without a matter counterpart, in other words it was pure energy with Divine patternings. As it began to slow down its vibrational frequency, matter began to coalesce from the pure energy patternings. The first matter that did coalesce was absolutely pure, as yet untainted by negative intrusions of human thought or feeling as we know it today." [...]
>
> This first matter was called Prima Matra by the ancients.
>
> The forms of Prima Matra we have existent today are less in vibrational frequency than the original Prima Matra, but powerful nonetheless for spiritual transformation and physical healing. [...]
>
> Tehuti / Thoth has impressed upon us that we simply cannot comprehend just how sacred this substance truly is.[3]

Grove then proceeds to describe *monoatomic gold (oro monatomico)*:

---

[3]   [https://www.bibliotecapleyades.net/montauk/esp_montauk_12a.htm]

> Monoatomics have been exhibiting the properties of superconductors at normal temperatures. The principle behind a superconductor is that it is able to carry electrical energy without any resistance present, thus exhibiting a zero loss in the conduction of that energy.[4]

This is subatomic physics, the realm covered in McTaggart's *The Field*. As for the "super conductive medium" just mentioned, that is, superconductivity, it is told by Simeon Nartoomid that the human body might have superconducting properties:

> It has been shown that the cells of the body communicate with each other as do superconductors [...] Superconductors are able to communicate or transfer energy to each other irrelevant of distance if their Meissner fields are in resonance.[5]

Again, like in McTaggart's book, we are given a scientific explanation of vril, etc.

Scalar energy is also often mentioned in conjunction with zero point energy. Scalar energy is supposedly present at each point in space.

A scalar *field* assigns a value to every point in space; on the other hand, in a *vector* field, every point has a vector consisting of a direction and a strength. Gravity in space can be defined by a vector field, as can the magnetic field surrounding a magnet.

---

4   Ibid.

5   Ibid.

Brian Dunning is a skeptic, but he does say the following about *scalar waves:*

> Scalar waves are the hypothetical electromagnetic waves propagating along this field; although, unlike conventional waves that propagate outward like ripples in a pond, scalar waves propagate through space longitudinally, like ocean waves breaking on a long straight beach. These scalar waves, also called Tesla waves or Maxwellian waves, are said to be the mechanism of zero–point energy. It should be stressed that this definition of scalar field theory is not supported by experiment or by any actual physics. […] It is true that Tesla did envision and describe superweapons capable of frying entire invading armies, but his concept was analogous to what we now call a directed energy weapon, basically a powerful particle beam. Tesla did also claim to have completed a partial unified field theory that unified gravity with electromagnetism, which is something that scalar field theory also claims.[6]

The scalar field supposedly has a fourth dimension.

Like the quintessence, the scalar field is dynamic.

Vril equates to direct electricity in the atmosphere...

I declare you omnium...!

Omnium is all, all is omnium.

---

[6]   https://skeptoid.com/episodes/4121

Universe is a flow of omnium waves.

All beings, animate and inanimate, are permeated by omnium.

Back in the day, Hugo Gernsback repeatedly asked Nikola Tesla to write a series of articles about his life. Eventually, the texts were published in Gernsback's *Electrical Experimenter*, February-October 1919. Later, the series of articles were collected in the book *My Inventions* (the following is based on the Swedish translation, *Mina uppfinningar*).

In Heinz Werner's preface, we read that Tesla believed in the ether as a medium for energy transfer and that he met Vivekānanda after the Parliament of World Religions in Chicago in 1893. Hindu physics is described by Werner as dealing with *Brahman*, the absolute, whose primary substance is *ākāśa*, space. Vivekānanda himself is said to have believed that ākāśa is

> The original state of all matter, the most subtle and omnipresent aspect of the manifested universe. Through the influence of prāṇa, ākāśa is set in a swirling motion and expresses itself as what we call matter.

By vorticular motion, the ether is activated. Tesla meant that *ether vortices, ether motions, ether currents* are the foundations of physics; by controlling the etheric vortices, man can gain access to free energy and become the lord of the universe.

Through the influence of vortexes, prima materia is set in motion – in swirling motion. The physicist is a Vortex Master ...! Once affected by vril, the ether is set in motion, in vorticular motion.

Tesla advocated the vortex as a primal form of energy – but it goes beyond that – for mystics claim that even the energy of man is spiral-shaped.

15. ASTRAL WAR REVISITED

The first two chapters of this book concern *the astral war* – the virtual fight going on since the beginning, even before recorded history. It is the battle between dark and light, with man's soul as the battlefield. Here we shall briefly reiterate some key points.

To repeat: the phrase "astral war" is a cosmic war raging since time immemorial, fought by the spiritual forces against the materialism of the Demiurge. In the current context, it can be seen as an "immaterial, mental, psychic" war fought by will-endowed humans against the rule of mindless nihilism, ultimately, a fight against the still extant force of the Demiurge.

Light against dark. Angels versus Demons. Devas versus Asuras. That is the struggle. Details aside, this must be clear to any conscious actor in today's operational reality.

Conversely, not knowing of this, not acknowledging the astral character of the fight we are in, will make you an early casualty of 21st century livelihood. Not knowing this will lead you toward mirages in the desert. The leaders you follow must embody more than vacuous materialism.

The "astral war" can also be regarded as a propaganda war, frequency war, energy war, magic war, cosmic war, holy war, psychic war, or culture war (*Kulturkampf*).

Whatever the label, this war is fought in immaterial realms – but – by *influxus*, it will affect the material realm.

The emphasis in the astral war is on "the immaterial realm," in 4D and beyond, in the astral world, Nirvana, and "Heaven." How, then, do we mortals, living in 3D, in material reality, fight this war? Since conceptual-mindful activities like "writing, speaking, and online research" are performed with a higher purpose, they can be seen as "astral warfare." The same applies to physical activities: if you are active in a topical movement, even if you actually serve in an army, this is also astral warfare on the side of the light, given this caveat: *as long as it is conceptually viable in the context of idealism versus materialism, it is viable in fighting the rule of the Demiurge.*

You could even say that *any* activity is part of the astral war. Work, leisure, and everything, if done with a pertinent purpose, are all enriching, strengthening you as a conscious, self-reliant being, impervious to the outreach of the Demiurge.

The idealism intimated can be of different kinds – but – at the very least, it has to acknowledge a person's Will, Thought, and Passion, and from them derivable values like courage, fidelity, self-restraint, reason, justice, and compassion. Not acknowledging this is collaborating with the enemy – the Demiurge.

No one is neutral in the astral war. Either you fight for freedom of thought, freedom of art, freedom of expression, and freedom for people, or you support the Demiurge. Wittingly or unwittingly.

The term "frequency war" was elaborated upon in *Actionism* (2017). This concept was created by David Wilcock, and it means that your soul, your mind, and your mood are part of the fight, whether you like it or not. For instance, if you start the day in an exuberant mood, then read about the "X number of dead in a remote war" – and if you are horrified by this, you become pessimistic, fearing the outbreak of WWIII or similar catastrophes. If this happens, you are a casualty of the frequency war. Mainstream media has succeeded in turning your current optimism into pessimism.

Not a single, tangible shot is fired at you in this. Instead, it is a war of nerves, of mental frequencies: a frequency war. According to Wilcock, a group he calls the Cabal deliberately acts this way; "they steal energy through sacrifice." Examples of this are the assassination of President Kennedy and 9/11, as Wilcock stated on the radio show "Fade to Black" in May 2014.

This is the nature of the Astral War. So, in short, acknowledge this and be successful in fighting it.

Again: there are no "non-combatants" in the astral war. Either you fight the tyranny of the Demiurge, or you surrender yourself to it.

Imagine, for instance, the film *We Were Soldiers* (1996), where the correspondent in the middle of the battlefield says, "I'm a non-combatant!" And Sam Eliot's sergeant says, "Ain't no such thing today," and hands him an M-16.

If you interpret this fight as spiritual and see the M-16 as a spiritual weapon, you have the gist of today's zeitgeist. That is how every individual should perceive the world. Not opting for neutral zones or safe spaces. Instead, being determined to fight – and win – the astral war. Defeat the rule of materialism and inaugurate a rule of spirit.

One could even say that *astral war* and *astral art* are virtually identical. Remember Swedish poet Edith Södergran: "The spirit of song is war."

The Astral warrior: His weapon: the word, His plan: holism, His symbol: the mandala.

Astral war, frequency war, energy war. Cold war in a country garden. War games, tin soldiers parading, propaganda war 24/7. Learn to love it – live it – forever at storming distance, forever mindfully burning with the burning magnesium in the sky, the illumination round lighting up a diameter of 800 m.

Astral war, holy war, total war. As intimated, it is not just about fighting mindfully. It might also include tangible fighting. This, of course, has to be done lawfully.

The use of combat similes in a "war of words" is as old as Moses. *Rally around the flag, gain ground, take commanding heights,* etc. Of course, you shouldn't take the combat zone analogy too far, though. However, it all depends on your overall mindset. As "The Law of One" series said, you have to offer at least 51% *service to others.* This is the moral litmus test. You don't have to be a saint, but you have to at least be 51% positively disposed towards your brethren.

Conversely, if you are predominantly (more than 51%) *service to self-disposed*, then you are on the dark side, and you need to be reeducated morally.

A man of the light may come in many sizes and shapes. What matters is if he mindfully fights the Demiurge.

Every freedom fighter must know the nature of the conflict – (1) the essentially astral/mental/immaterial character of it, and (2) that it is a war, a total war, an unforgiving struggle. The first must be acknowledged by the all-too "run-of-the-mill, formal, academic" dissident, the one thinking that the materialist regime will go down simply by informing people about it, showing statistics and teaching of things like "the medical benefits of being occupied with culture (and not material pleasures)." Simply being right will not bring victory. Facts also have a symbolic character and must be presented wisely in this respect, presented in a proactive, willful, energetic fashion.

The second feature (astral war as total war) has to be acknowledged by the "new age hippie" guided by memes like "let love rule." While it is true that we all have the light inside (the ability for love and compassion), acknowledging this doesn't mean that you should be so paralyzed with compassion that you can't fight an evil power.

Assess the target. You can't fight armored units with swords. And you can't fight the Demiurge, primeval darkness, the Prince of Darkness himself, with "statistics, journalism, and sociology." You have to fight him with astral weapons – astral light – will-endowed thought, imbued in light.

These are the characteristics of an astral warrior:

- Offering at least 51% of your service to others.
- Having the ability to meditate, using willpower, thinking constructively (and not applying fear-based thinking).
- Having the I AM impulse, acknowledging this inner light.

Conversely, he shouldn't be orientated towards the dark side, governed by fear and desire, or a materialist. *Actionism – How to Become a Responsible Man* discusses morality further.

The astral war is not fought by way of debate, deliberation, and discursive thought. It is fought by way of initiation, inspiration, and inebriation.

The storm is gathering – the Mother of all Battles, astral variety – a battle of resurrection and restoration, resurgence and reanimation, reformation and return – a return to sanity and spirituality, creativity and exuberance, and justice for all.

In the astral war, you need people who truly believe. You need people with what the Germans call *Glaubenskraft* – the power of faith. Conversely, you can't fight it with mentally weak people, people succumbing to their material desires.

The astral war is a fight of light against darkness. The light can be virtually "weaponized" by being imbued by every lightworker's will and thought. The enemy also uses this strain of virtual weaponizing. In many different instances, the dark is weaponized. For example, porn is weaponized degeneracy, and "safe spaces/trigger warnings" are weaponized emotionalism.

This is what we face. In this, the freedom fighter must will the light, will the victory. You can't oppose the dark with mere "acceptance." You must want to drive the Spear of Destiny through its heart.

It will take time to depolarize the primeval darkness. However, in this battle, you must understand that every light-imbued will counts.

Weaponize your spirituality. Become a virtual warrior monk.

Attack your enemies with it. Ask them, "Why don't YOU go and nurture your spiritual being, reconnect with the creator of your soul, your spiritual father." This could silence them because the very existence of a soul scares them.

"People shudder before the holy mildness as before an attack on their lives," as poet Bertil Malmberg said.

The astral war is about an initiation into a higher vibration.

16. ASTRAL ART

Beyond the mere message, an astral warrior has to know how to express himself with flair and pizazz. In the eternal struggle between Devas and Asuras, the former were the artistically gifted ones, and this, to some extent, is mirrored below.

Astral war and *astral art* are akin, as I stated previously, "You could say that *astral war* and *astral art* virtually are the same thing. Remember Swedish poet Edith Södergran: 'The spirit of song is war.'"

Style matters, even in the astral war.

Art, culture, and other activities directed by the muses – literature, painting, song – this realm often becomes unfairly treated in esoteric circumstances. It is neglected because it is not so easy to systemize. My novel *Antropolis* (2009, in Swedish only) is about this – how in a *Kulturkampf* of esotericism versus materialism, in the astral war of idealism versus mindlessness, the idealist camp often forgets that *art* is the most effective way of defeating the mindless forces. Devas inspire art; Asuras inspire technology.

This pattern might be simplistic, but it has to be remembered.

Not all technology is bad – but – if left to roam free, technology will make this world into a desert. The musical forces, art, and culture must always be there to posit an alternative.

The spontaneous strain, the unconditioned, the creative forces must always make a stand against the workings of blind necessity. This strain of *musical spontaneity* in man must be acknowledged, nurtured, and allowed to function, or else man will not thrive at all.

Thus, the astral warrior, the differentiated astral actor, must never forget Deva's alternative – the non-existent path, "the path even undreamed of by the greatest utopians" – the way of the artist, the musical path, the path is sung as you go forth – akin to the *Dreamtime* means of communications, the *Songlines* Chatwin spoke of. It is a path conquering necessity and destiny, the impossible conquering the possible, the proactive defeating the reactive.

This goes beyond ordinary initiation. The astral warrior cannot solely be led by rituals, texts, and practices. They might be a start, but in the final instance, he is alone. He is the artist before his canvas, the author before his empty page. Everything depends on him. "That I live, on this everything depends," as Meister Eckart said. For the artist, everything depends on him creating the glorified artwork – the magnum opus – the revelation to reveal all secrets, all history, and all in one and one in all.

The astral war cannot be fought by looking at programs, instructions, and existing patterns. True, you might need some formal preparation – as in, you can't have total rookies in the front line – but – in essence, in the final battle, everything has to be conceived of intuitively. In the ongoing astral war, every situation is created new, in this instance, by the very activities of the forces of light, singing forth their way as they go.

The activist taking his recourse to known facts, patterns, and threat perceptions will be overrun and defeated in no time. Instead, the real astral warrior fights like a hurricane, like a lightning bolt out of the blue, unpredictable as dice, free and fluent like water.

The activist, not knowing that his soul (his feelings, his conceptions, his mindset, his Self, etc.) is the battlefield of the astral war, is like a person during WWII not understanding that there is no safe space behind the front. The whole territory is part of the area of operation, like cities being targets for bombs.

The astral war is a propaganda war. Both sides must acknowledge this, even the forces of light. You can't be ambivalent, nor should you begin your "propaganda fight" by obsessing over words. "Good style is equal to having something to say," as Matthew Arnold had it. This is the fundamental principle. You must have a message – in this case, promoting light instead of dark because light is information and creativity. Darkness is the absence of information and sclerosis. However, you must also be able to present this in a memorable way. To promulgate propaganda is about knowing how to handle language, to know the value of words, and the nuances of synonyms. Still, not all lightworkers and freedom fighters know this!

Indeed, everything is decided within, yet there is still so much we can express about the spiritual and divine invisible world with our all-too-human languages. For example, take these synonyms for *esoteric*:

Arcane, mystical, mystic, hermetic, hidden, inner, occult, profound, secret, Sibylline.

Likewise, for *divine*, there is: angelic, spiritual, eternal, heavenly, holy, transcendent, anointed, consecrated, hallowed, exalted, sanctified, beatific, blissful, glorious, godly, omniscient, sacramental, sacrosanct, transmundane.

Finally, for *pious*, we have: saintly, devout, sanctimonious, devoted, reverent, sacred, priestly.

This illustrates that language does matter. Furthermore, some new-age types of people have a rather flat, tepid language. Judging by channelings, even angels seem to have a certain bureaucratic–technical strain in their expression. Of course, you shouldn't obsess about it too much. It is the content that counts, not the form. However, those who are literate, and don't view life with closed eyes, can formulate themselves beyond "God, Love, Oneness."

There is a responsibility to explain what is going on in a legible manner and with a varied vocabulary.

To make a lasting impression in the astral world, we must formulate ourselves as astrally prominent – with depth, flair, and style.

This is within reach for us human beings. It is possible that even the angels might express themselves a bit formalistic and tepid. In a way, that is the divine condition. It is elevated beyond the lust and anguish of the human realm; it is elevated beyond passion and color. It *can* be (and sometimes is) the human receiving the divine influxus, the human channel, the human seer and prophet, that has to add vibrance and flair to their visions.

Even the human being Orpheus impressed the gods with his song.

In any case, we must express the divine in all its diversity, not just by saying, "God is love." In Deepak Chopra's *How to Know God* (2000), Chopra tries to portray God and the divine in more than one way; he sees this complex as an integral phenomenon. For instance, the aspects of study, fascination, concentrated meditation, and devotional joy, to name but a few, are covered in the book. The foreword also references a wise man who praised Chopra for widening the concept of God. He took it beyond the hippie movement's nowadays trite, "God is love."

We must go beyond "God is love"! Indeed, we have to acknowledge the compassion and love of God – but – there is so much more to it. In theology, for instance, they speak about the *numinous* side of God, the fearful side. Any god worthy of its name has a wrathful aspect; this is true of Jehova, Siva, Viṣṇu, Odin, Zeus, and many others. All gods embody the principle of "*numen tremendum et fascinosum*" (Latin: fearful and fascinating power).

To convey this, we need real and artful language, for example, the works of the English mystic William Blake. In the poem "Milton," he envisioned the creative sun god Los at war with the atrophied Synagogue of Satan. Of the equally creative, life-affirming yet fearful "Children of Los," it is said:

> These are the Children of Los; thou seest the Trees on mountains,
> The winds blow heavy, loud they thunder thro' the darksome sky,
> Uttering prophecies & speaking instructive words to the sons
> Of men: These are the Sons of Los: These are the Visions of Eternity,
> But we see only as it were the hem of their garments
> When without vegetable eyes we view these wonderous Visions. ["Milton," Book the First]

In the prologue to the poem, we also have this, which is strikingly apt as a call to astral war:

> Bring me my Bow of burning gold:
> Bring me my Arrows of desire:
> Bring me my Spear: O clouds unfold!
> Bring me my Chariot of fire.
>
> I will not cease from Mental Fight,
> Nor shall my Sword sleep in my hand
> Till we have built Jerusalem
> In England's green & pleasant land.

That is how you fight the Demiurge – with authority, power, and aesthetic flare. Another poet who embodies this is the Finnish-Swedish poet Edith Södergran (1892-1923), who wrote the following on the astral war:

> All superstition I want to sweep out with a silent broom,
> all pettiness I will mockingly kill.
> Upon the head of The Snake I mount, stinging it with my sword.
> O you my good sword, which I have received from heaven, I kiss you.
> You shall not rest
> until the Earth is a garden, where the gods dream by wonderful goblets.

This is "Mystery" from *Framtidens skugga* ("Shadow of the Future," 1920); from her collected poems (*Samlade dikter*), translated by me, from my essay *Borderline* which contains a chapter about the holistic, mystic strains of Södergran. Two other poems quoted in that article are the following, pertinent to astral combat. The first describes a boat ride down a violent current:

> There you stand, a hero with newborn blood.
> enraptured in tranquility, a bonfire of reflective ice,
> as if the commandment of death wasn't written for you:
> blessed waves bring your keel forward.
> ["Vortex of Madness" ("Vanvettets virvel"), 1918]

"Enraptured in tranquility" is a perfect way of describing the mindset of an astral warrior: perfectly calm yet perfectly alert. Then we have this from the same collection, *The September Lyre* ("Septemberlyran"):

> Mars helmets in the mist...
> Clients sitting down by overturned tables.
> Strangers rule the world...
> Higher, more beautiful, godlike. ["The Tempest" ("Stormen"), 1918]

Södergran was the one who said, "The spirit of song is war." This is the heart of the "astral war, astral art" phenomenon. Can you find writers that express the same warlike musical tones? It is not easy in the framework of a materialist mindset when war is associated with destruction and suffering. However, the astral war is a war of liberation, of throwing off the yoke of the Demiurge. No struggle can be nobler.

Previously in this chapter, I spoke of God and the need to see God more than a benevolent hippy god, a one-dimensional emanation of love. Again, God is compassionate, but to merely see God as love leads to paralysis, permissiveness, and indulgence in optimism. Now, I wouldn't go so far as to say, as Spengler did, that "optimism is cowardice" (in *Man and Technics,* 1932), but the current paradigm needs widening, elaboration, and clarification, not by making it transparent but by making it more complex. We need texts like Carlos Castaneda's books, brimming over with numinous aspects of the astral world. Like in book one of the series,

The Teachings of Don Juan, when neophyte student Castaneda, in a drug-induced trance, meets the peyote god Mescalito.

To simply quote the passage wouldn't quite capture the numinous aspect, but suffice to say, that this is about as close as you get to revelation in modern fiction.

Revelation is what we need, an approach to godhead. Where do we get this apart from the Bible, Sanskrit Purāṇas, Gnostic scriptures, and other classic texts? We might be able to diversify the approach by listening to figures who claim to offer advice from beings like Metatron, Quan Yin, Pallas Athena, and Helios. Of course, you need discernment when approaching these alleged "words of god," but as intimated in the foreword of this study, this is a mixture of critical evaluation and intuitive realization – so, from my perspective, don't dismiss new age spirituality outright, explore it for nuggets of truth.

New-age people may also learn the need to study ancient languages and scriptures from "the traditional schoolist," to give them a more variegated vocabulary to express the divine. On the other hand, traditional mystics could gain some actuality and contemporaneity from the new-age community. *Influxus* from the divine world didn't just stop in Year Zero, the beginning of the Christian Era. Not all truths can be found by looking at ancient scriptures. Take, for instance, *The Law of One* series, mentioned in Chapter 15. Is it really so incredible that this, as stated in the book proper, is a channeling of the entity known as Ra in Egyptian mythology?

You can't dismiss it outright. You have at least to read the book before you can evaluate it.

If you are an adept with an esoteric worldview, acknowledging that there are higher realities beyond our material, 3D reality, then you can't systematically dismiss every claim about contact with higher worlds. You can't say that *you* are the last judge in every esoteric matter because then you would, for sure, be god.

A modicum of openness is required when approaching the astral combat zone. You go to war as you go to wisdom, as Castaneda said: with fear, determination, respect, and wide-awake apprehension.

Regarding "Astral war as astral art," what other invigorating quotes have we to arouse the spiritual ranks? In the Bible, New Testament, we do have some lines worthy of quoting. For example, Christ "with power and authority" teaches his seventy sent-out disciples how to behave:

> 'And heal the sick there, and say to them, 'The kingdom of God has come near to you.' But whatever city you enter, and they do not receive you, go out into its streets and say, 'The very dust of your city which clings to us we wipe off against you. Nevertheless know this, that the kingdom of God has come near you.' But I say to you that it will be more tolerable in that Day for Sodom than for that city. Woe to you, Chorazin! Woe to you, Bethsaida! For if the mighty works which were done in you had been done in Tyre and Sidon, they would have

repented long ago, sitting in sackcloth and ashes. But it will be more tolerable for Tyre and Sidon at the judgment than for you. And you, Capernaum, who are exalted to heaven, will be brought down to Hades. He who hears you hears Me, he who rejects you rejects Me, and he who rejects Me rejects Him who sent Me.' Then the seventy returned with joy, saying, 'Lord, even the demons are subject to us in Your name.' And He said to them, 'I saw Satan fall like lightning from heaven. Behold, I give you the authority to trample on serpents and scorpions, and over all the power of the enemy, and nothing shall by any means hurt you.' [Luke 10:9–19]

This quote is sufficient to remind everyone that Christ was no "hugging hippie." He preached with authority, and he envisioned a fierce struggle. For instance, in Matthew 24, Jesus predicted the destruction of the Temple, saying,

> "Do you not see all these things? Assuredly, I say to you, not one stone shall be left here upon another, that shall not be thrown down."). And he drove the merchants from the temple, people selling things on holy ground, Jesus saying: "It is written, 'My house shall be called a house of prayer,' but you have made it a 'den of thieves.'" [Matthew 21:13]

Astral war is astral art. The *Kulturkampf* of today is an art form in itself. So even if it is a total war without the possibility of remaining neutral, the astral war still has its charm. "The spirit of song is war," as Södergran said. Art is an operation, "an emotional intelligence operation." And a fine symbol for "art as an operation" is a "music band on tour." I personally haven't been on tour, as I am not a musician, but I can relate to this peculiar state of being when it is conveyed in songs like *Wherever I May Roam* (Metallica), *Telegram* (Nazareth), *Far, Far Away* (Slade) and *Thunder Road* (Judas Priest). It is about Actionist concepts like "movement as a state" and "action raising you mentally," an indescribable kind of trance, of super-meditation while active.

As for the simile of "intelligence operation," I come to think of Peter Wright's *Spy Catcher* where this MI5 officer speaks of operations intermeshing, one going into the other, no end in sight, just "movement as a state" – a term he doesn't employ – but – this is the case for any operational professional. You have to know "movement as a state," you have to incorporate it into your being. After that, you'll learn to manage and maybe even love the specificity of the astral war.

To conclude this chapter, here is a quote from the Old Testament, Psalm 46: "Be still and know that I am God / I will be exalted among the nations / I will be exalted in the Earth!"

This highlights the "I AM" saying that Rudolf Steiner noted as central to Christianity. When God says "I AM," this is his prerogative as the foundation of existence – and later, the Logos of God, Christ, was incarnated in human form, making his seven "I AM" statements ("I am the light of the world, I am the door, I am the way, the truth, and the life" etc., q.v. The Gospel of John). Therefore, every pious man or astral warrior can say I AM and acknowledge the affinity between his soul and the All Soul. Thus, I AM is the very formula for *ethics founded in metaphysics,* the most succinct formula of this kind you can find. You can read more about this in *Borderline* and *Actionism.*

Finally, we bring this chapter to a conclusion with another Old Testament quote for the astral war.

> "O Lord, our Lord, how excellent is thy name in all the Earth!" [Psalm 8] – This is a line to strengthen and guide every true astral warrior – as is, "though I walk through the valley of the shadow of death, I will fear no evil; For You are with me; Your rod and Your staff, they comfort me." [Psalm 23]

17. INTEGRATING OPPOSITES

The subject of "integrating opposites," the integral perspective of not seeing everything in black and white, is vital for the astral warrior. Of course, a freedom fighter has to fight for the light – but – having affirmed his pure intent, he must also venture into the vast liminal areas that exist and learn from them in order to become a more fully evolved Self.

Thus, you might ask the astral warrior: how are you doing in your spirituality? Are you becoming too complacent? Too safe in your acknowledgment of life and light?

An element of risk might be required. *You're hungry for heaven, but you need a little hell,* as it were. Of course, you shouldn't do anything stupid, like harming or alienating your friends. The "integral perspective" I present here is not about living in sin and misery!

Instead, we need some sagacity here. We need a modicum of common spiritual sense in this act of brinkmanship. What we seek to portray has some affinity to the need for *atheism as cleansing,* as Simone Weil had it. Imagine standing in hell with no way home, no god, no nothing. That is the kind of virtual hell the all-too-pious man needs to contemplate.

It is about integrating the opposites and balancing out the poles. It is not about expressly reversing the role of God and the Devil, as William Blake sometimes did. It is about acknowledging that "no tree can grow to heaven unless its roots reach down to hell" (Jung). There is an exquisite poetic rendering of this by Bertil Malmberg (1889-1958), a Swedish Academy member. In "Lord Lucifer Calls the Creator" ("Hertig Lucifer anropar skaparen" in *Under månens fallande båge,* 1947), he gives the dichotomy a fertile ground in the form of Lucifer addressing God, by saying that the elevated Lord requires the intensity of the lower regions to remain whole:

> If you take your hand from me
> God
> if you let me fall
> then with me falls
> half your being.
> Beauty might not die:
> it lives on
> as an ideal pattern
> an elevated shape
> but it doesn't sound.
> Never more from the depths
> of existence shuddering lust

will rise.

Lord, consider well

before you abandon me.

Venture out into the grey area! Elsewhere in his poetry, Malmberg hints at a plagued existence, tempted by mindless sprites to join them and glide with them in moonlit climes forever, forgetting his shape and name and being a shadow among shadows ("Vanvettets lockelse," "The Allure of Insanity," 1927).

This is reminiscent of H. P. Lovecraft, his American contemporary (1890-1937), envisioning joining the flitting floc of specters in the night. However, Malmberg managed to fuse his shadowy side with a vision of divine light. The collection *Dikter vid gränsen* (*Poems at the Edge,* 1935) ostensibly was about the apocalyptic strains of the times, about the degenerate culture of the west and how "everything has gone to the dogs and ruin" as Theognis once said. It was an epic, prophetic poem synthesizing man, God, and history – but – in the middle of the collection was also a section of poems about the poet's self, his timeless metaphysical-ethical deliberations, which again incorporated the theme of being tempted by the dark side (prose translation):

> It is like not being a carnal Son of Man – merely an ill-fated, uncertain, irresponsible demon – like merely carrying a shadowy baggage – like my human likeness being but camouflage.

The poet is dragged away into misty nights of pale moonlight amid chaotic grey vistas of fluttering wings. He wants to steel himself against the irresponsible existence implied by this – but – he also acknowledges that half of his being belongs in this twilight zone. If he denies it, it still discreetly returns. It is a constant subtext in his life, his dreams, and all his efforts. Until, finally, he obtains the poetic synthesis (again, a prose rendering):

> I want to love the light, defend clarity; live my daily life with order and law; but neither deny the grey, Hadean pallor. I am both Son of Man and demon. And between two worlds I must build a bridge.

This is *integral spirituality* par preference, rendered in distinct lines of deathless beauty. And in a more formal, scholarly vein, the same syndrome is envisioned by Carl Jung (1875-1961), who spoke about the need for a tree to have its roots in hell to grow into heaven. In *Borderline,* I said this about Jung's way of *integrating the opposites.* Jung spoke about *individuation* as a way of becoming whole, about uniting with God. And...

> [...] to the random esotericist this sounds good. Let's be whole, let's unite with God. But to reach this sublime state you have to walk a long road, it would seem. It is not done by simply kneeling, saying a prayer and be saved. Individuation is a process. Wikipedia says that individuation is 'the psychological process of integrating the opposites, including the conscious with the unconscious, while still

maintaining their relative autonomy.' Further, individuation is about uniting the individual unconscious with the collective unconscious. All this sounds like an integrative approach in sync with the *Borderline* project. But at this stage, you might also have to ask yourself if you really want to take such a ride, delving into the individuation process. What's it really like to dive into the depths of your unconscious with all its fears, nightmares and demons? What's it like to live in humanity's unconscious and meet all the horrors of history and myth? It is all there and in the Jungian way of knowledge there is the need to encounter them and acknowledge them. Discernment is required when wishing to integrate all the opposites of the Inner Mind. In the Jungian Way of Knowledge you have to admit that you yourself have less attractive traits. This is symbolized by the Shadow, a figure representing suppressed and taboo-related sides of your being. It is having to admit that you're 'less than perfect,' that you too can have less appealing traits to your character. The trick here is to acknowledge this and move on to your goal, not indulging in darkness per se but realizing that *la condition humaine* is complex. It is not simply about 'being good, avoiding bad'. Ideals we must have but the Jungian attitude of integrating opposites is a step on the way of knowing ourselves more profoundly. –*Gnôthi seauvtón*, know thyself; this was the inscription on the Apollo temple in Olympia. [Svensson 2015, p 146]

Know yourself by seeking the truth, even if it takes you to the gates of hell. The coda of William Blake's "The Marriage of Heaven and Hell" is: "Without contraries is no progression. Attraction and Repulsion, Reason and Energy, Love and Hate, are necessary to Human existence."

It also says: "[E]very thing that lives is Holy." Every living being has energy, from the atom to the archangels. In *Borderline*, I said this on the subject:

> Everything in the Universe is connected, everything is energy. God is energy, man by way of his spirit is energy. All separate entities are energy, even the inanimate objects. Remember the formula $E=MC2$, 'energy equals mass times the speed of light to the power of two.' Everything is energy, even the tiniest speck of dust; there are no lifeless objects, and there is no space devoid of energy, forcefields or particles. 'The perfect vacuum' is a mere theoretical concept. – Speaking of modern physics, this has also learned us that energy can't be destroyed, it can only change form. This is the principle of the conservation of energy, there to be used as a 'natural science proof of God' if you so choose. [ibid p 211]

One could say that any creed worthy of its name has an integral character. We implied this when speaking about gods in the previous chapter: all true gods have a numinous side to them (Odin, Siva, Zeus). In the mythopoetic sphere, when it comes to artists expressing a *Weltanschauung*, they have to balance the poles and integrate the opposites, as was the case with Malmberg, Blake, Södergran, Castaneda, and even Lovecraft occasionally. Then, we have less successful attempts, such as Oscar Wilde (1854-1900). It is true that he was unfairly treated by society, but his overall vision lacks something. In his early phase, he was all "enjoy yourself, cherish art and the muses, fall for temptations," and in his late phase (q.v. "De Profundis"), he was all "penance, a poor sinner, quietism is the way." It becomes rather bipolar, unsatisfying from the views of both aesthetics-as-ethics and integrating opposites. However, when he was in good shape as an author, he actually integrated the opposites rather well, as was evident in works like *The Picture of Dorian Gray, The Sphinx,* and *Salome.*

For a cursory view of "integrated writers," read *Borderline* with its renderings of Nietzsche, Södergran, Castaneda, Jung, and T. S. Eliot. I can't quote it all here. However, I will quote from the book concluding the chapter with an integral attitude to art and stating that the very nature of art is to integrate the opposites and to reach "harmony through conflict."

> *[A]rt is the striving for harmony through conflict.* In order to reach artistic harmony you have to stage a conflict of some kind – like the individual versus the collective, action versus contemplation, male versus female, East versus West etc. etc. – The impulse to this idea per se, this way of looking at art, is from the concept of 'The Seven Rays,' for instance discussed by Alice Bailey (1880–1949). This is an esoteric way of structuring the different moods, attitudes and energies of man, and the

fourth ray in this system is that of the artist. And the motto for him was, indeed, 'harmony through conflict.' [ibid p 194]

There are many prime examples of this, for instance, in the songs of Judas Priest. The very name of that group symbolizes the fusing of light and shade. In the lyrics, there are both hymns and hellish vistas, along with pieces fusing it all, both lyrically and musically. Other heavy metal groups that successfully fused light and shade are Black Sabbath, Led Zeppelin, and Iron Maiden. Conversely, no musician or artist can merely portray either bright or dark climes. They must fuse them and provide each realm its due. Also, while acknowledging the need for "the whole gamut," an artist shouldn't strive for holistic integration in every song, every line, or every note. In another quote from the same chapter, it is stated thus:

In the true artwork both light and dark are along, conducting a coexistence. And as an advice to the budding artist, I'd say, don't expressly try to mix them in the same scene, in the same line, in the same breath. Explore the possibilities of each mood at its proper place. This, for its part, is one of many aesthetical tips Ingmar Bergman (1918-2007) delivers in his autobiography *Laterna Magica* (1987). [ibid p 196]

We have now ventured into the lands of "integral spirituality," of "deepening the god image," of "fusing light and shade into a higher amalgam" in order to portray the astral war. It is risky to embrace the darkness in a fight against the Demiurge, the Lord of Darkness. However, it is about seeking combat similes for the astral struggle; it doesn't entail outright destruction, smoking ruins, scarcity, and regimentation of the whole society. When portraying the astral war, we, of course, have to use similes from fighting and warring of any kind, even the physical kind.

In a similar vein, one mustn't be afraid to venture into the grey zone to perfect one's astral armor. There are "vast grey areas in between" the dark and the light. As long as you know that you fight for the light, freedom, creativity, and development versus sclerosis, coercion, and necessity, and as long you provide "at least 51% Service to Others," then you can safely approach the gates of Hell and knock on them in the quest for truth.

18. THREE ASTRAL WAR ASPECTS

Astral War Today

The astral war has raged since the beginning of time when man's souls were enveloped in corporeal bodies and in the material reality of dualism.

Parallel to this, humanity has always strived to return to spiritual realms, Nirvana, and godhead. Terminology pertains to this: the fall into corporeality is the *involution*, and the way back to godhead is the true *evolution*.

This might sound simple and clear-cut, but there are aspects of it that need to be discussed. For instance, will all of humanity evolve, transcend materiality, and aim for heaven? I doubt this will be the case. A large part of humanity is not inclined toward spiritualism. They are trapped in atheistic negativity.

Thus, humanity is facing "the great divide." On the one hand, we have mystics acknowledging the existence of the soul and that reality is structured in layers from 3D and up, becoming more immaterial as they begin the ascent. On the other hand, we have atheists denying the spiritual side and concentrating on material reality, reducing everything to sensory perception and denying the capacity of intuition.

However, "great divide" or not, human civilization has gained an increased element of "idealism, conceptuality, mentality." Ideas and abstract concepts play a larger role today than in the past. Fourth-Generation Warfare presents the theory that today's conflicts are not merely focused on regular forces in combat but also on psychological warfare, especially through media manipulation and lawfare. The last concept is about using law as a weapon, such as delegitimizing the enemy through a legal process. "Media manipulation" obviously concerns propaganda. It is about portraying blue forces as saints and red forces as demons from hell or vice versa.

If Fourth-Generation Warfare is the war of today, it also has tangible elements in the form of terrorist attacks and guerillas. The element of propaganda is the most important one, however. In the successive major, all-out wars from the 30 Years War through to the Coalition Wars and WWI and WWII, propaganda has played an increasing role and now is more intense than ever.

The wars fought today are less intense, but every single shot is mythologized beyond belief, given media spin so that the common news consumer thinks that Armageddon is nigh.

This is modern war, propaganda war, an astral war regarding world events of a warlike kind. It is not about what actually happens. It is about what people *believe* happens.

So, how to rectify this? How to turn people away from letting their souls be the battlefield of this war?

As intimated, it is nearly useless to say to people that a single 7.62 cartridge fired in a MENA desert doesn't mean that WWIII is looming.

Again, it is about the Great Divide. Negative people will always be hooked on this kind of news. However, finally, when mankind at large is ready to create "paradise on Earth," these other people could be allowed to translocate to a grand-scale, parallel world VR simulation to live out the remains of their negativism, duality, and fear. The rest of mankind can then create their spiritual civilization without disturbance.

Astral War Myths

To the modern mind, "myth" means "a lie, something made up." However, in a more archaic, holistic vein, "myth" is golden. A story that has been labeled as myth has "graduated" – it has become immortal, an astral world narrative, a dreamworld story. A legend.

In this respect, myths are 4D stories that possess a soul. Conversely, stories merely pertaining to 3D are conditioned, "all too human," and banal.

Where, then, do we find tales pertaining to the astral war? Where are the inspirational stories about the forces of light fighting the Demiurge? To begin with, there is a story by Robert A. Heinlein, the novella *Lost Legacy* (anthologized in *Assignment in Eternity*, 1953). It is about a group of academics feeling fenced in by reductionist psychology. They discover anomalies in the concept and then become spiritual adepts fighting the cabal of materialist, nihilist operators ruling the land.

The group in question challenges behaviorism, the "man-machine" paradigm. Next, they venture into esotericism, learn about will controlling thought, and they become spiritual supermen. It is a bit simplistic. However, it is an example of a Science Fiction story explaining this in such a succinct and readable manner. In *Science Fiction Seen from the Right* I said that Heinlein, with this story,

> [...] can be seen as an informal teacher of esotericism – indeed, even better, a myth-maker for the coming golden age of spirituality, depicting as he does how the group our trio joins gets embroiled in a psychic struggle all over the land, a fight between the forces of Light and Dark. This is unique – because, fiction on the theme of spiritual elevation and the fight between will-powered Light and desire-driven Darkness, is a rare thing indeed, in and out of the SF field. However, maybe Edward Bulwer–Lytton in *The Coming Race* (1871) and Frederick S. Oliver in *A Dweller on Two Planets* (1905) come close to the dramatic spirituality of *Lost Legacy*. [Svensson 2016, p 24–25]

Another equally pertinent story is C. S. Lewis's *That Hideous Strength* (1947). It has the same theme of determined, Responsible Men fighting chauvinist nihilism. And, as well as *Lost Legacy* was rooted in the post-war USA, *That Hideous Strength* captures post-war England with some charm. It is about a university being forced to give way to a modern research institute. It is about an old wood, Merlin, and a spiritual leader in the form of the space-farer Elwin Ransom, known from Lewis's Science Fiction sagas *Out of the Silent Planet* and *Perelandra*, to which *That Hideous Strength* forms a finale.

In *Science Fiction Seen from the Right* I wrote that Lewis's book, was above *1984* and *Brave New World*, two other British novels which discussed the nature of nihilism. I said that these two novels,

> [...] tend to indulge in the evil, antagonistic sides of the plot while Lewis's novel along with showing us evil shows us a way out. Lewis has balanced the incredible with the eminently relatable. Orwell's and Huxley's novels were dramatically credible in stressing how "the enemy is well organized" but Lewis, in showing the power of The Common People, of the echo in medieval vaults and of acknowledging the Light, is more relevant to the era of Sat Yuga we live in today, the Era of Truth following on the Iron Age of Kali Yuga having just ended. [Svensson 2016, p. 57]

This is very important. In fighting evil, you can't just indulge in the fight per se. You have to have a vision of what to replace it with. To merely fight evil and praise victory over it is equal to *power positivism.* This merely leads to you becoming another tyrant.

The vertical dimension is always important. To acknowledge that reality is structured from "less real" to "more real" is essential for any worldview. If not, then everything gets embroiled in relativism, in the social, *horizontal* dimension, the realm of "human, all too human."

As we saw above, the Heinlein and Lewis stories in question had this perspective. Their heroes fought the Demiurge with an ontologically rooted ethic.

They were, indeed, astral warriors.

For further examples of astral war myth, there are the stories of Philip K. Dick. He didn't describe clear-cut astral fights, but he did approach other key elements of the struggle, such as acknowledging the Gnostic perspective of souls being caught in the material world and acknowledging esotericism and God.

Dick's opus is complex, and I portrayed it in *Science Fiction Seen from the Right.* This excerpt captures the gist of it, of Dick first writing the novel *Galactic Pot-Healer* in 1968, about an unhappy man being approached by a god. Then virtually the same thing happens in Dick's everyday reality, in 1974, portrayed in the novel *VALIS* (1981). This novel gives you a *theophany,* a vision of God:

> This is authoritative esotericism. This is Swedenborg in his Dream Diary, "The Ecstasy of Saint Teresa," Isaiah seeing "new heavens

and a new Earth." It is incomparable in its vision of the divine, of Being, of That Which Is, that which ontologically can't be questioned. It is supreme bliss and rest.

VALIS is a *relatable* theophany. The best of Dick's opus was "serious fiction in popular form," and this gloriously applies to *VALIS*, which provides both a story and a mystic's vision of the world. The appendix has a 52-paragraph, 15-page philosophical statement, a summary of Dick's Gnostic studies and divine experience.

VALIS emphasizes the fact that the battlefield of the astral war is you and your soul. *VALIS* is the story of a man in agony, and the divine experience doesn't enlighten and enliven him, not at first. Rather, he regrets having been illuminated by the divine light and then being left out in the cold, as the divine experience cools off, as it were. With time, after Dick had digested his 1974 experience more fully, he became more placid and tranquil, more "spiritual."

That being said, *VALIS* can be a trying read, going through all of Dick's interpretations and misinterpretations of his experience – but – all things considered, it has value as a document of a divine experience. Like Swedenborg's *Dream Diary*, it is also about a man in agony, haunted by visions that, in the end, illuminated and elevated its recipient.

Astral War Tactics

The "astral war" concept didn't begin with *Actionism – How to Become a Responsible Man*. However, *Actionism* used the term "frequency war," which is the same as astral war. So *Actionism* could be seen as a virtual astral war handbook for the keen individual.

"How shall I live?" This is the timeless question of morality. *Actionism* answered this. It provides the same ontological background as the book you're reading, that of God being a fusion of light-imbued will, thought, and passion. As fragments of the divine light, we soul-endowed humans must sum up our will and let it guide thought. Additionally, we must affirm the role of passion for giving the whole operation color and vitality, warmth, and compassion.

The role of the will is paramount. Hitherto, excepting Nietzsche, it has been virtually eradicated from the realm of ethics as a central concept. *Actionism* wants to change this by stressing that will, pure will, always is free. It spontaneously chooses light. Conversely, "a bound will" equals desire and indulging in darkness.

There must be an end to deliberation on "whether there is free will or not." By recourse to a perspective of "a hierarchy of realities," ethics can stand alone. Will is free, will is divine. Sum up your will and let it guide thought; let will fuse with thought into a higher amalgam of Will-Thought. Do this, and you will become a spiritual superman. This is the virtual astral war armor.

What more can be said concerning "astral war armor, astral war tactics, astral war survival for the common operator?" Only a remark on the latter wording and stress that in this war, there are no "common operators," no "random observers," and the like. Conscious presence is the only ideal, and mindful engagement is the only way. To sit by and think that things will rectify themselves is not an option. The battlefield is you, and you must stick to the program.

One piece of general advice for fighting the frequency war is from Saul Alinsky: "*a good tactic is one that you and your friends enjoy.*" This highlights the element of inspiration, creative joy, and spiritual uplifting that must be present when fighting the astral war and fighting the Demiurge. Conversely, activities that drain your energy must be avoided.

Details aside, since the battlefield is you, every emotion, every breath, every single nano-second of your existence counts. Sum up your will, take a deep, gentle breath, and say I AM – so you're ready for anything.

This creed can be summarized as *holism, intuition, and will-driven ethics.* As for the first term, holism, it is about seeing wholes, the big picture. For its part, *Borderline* explored holistic science, art, and ethics – and advocated against reductionism on the scientific level. To reduce phenomena into cases possible to study in a controlled situation might give us mastery of material nature, but it will not provide an ontologically viable worldview.

Aspects like these (holistic science, art, and ethics) were covered in *Borderline.* Concerning the reductionist-holistic dichotomy into the realm of astral war, the goal is to not fall into reductionist patterns when venturing into mythical realms and studying gods, myths, and legends. To reduce a god into "social factors" is madness; it applies a horizontal, human, conditioned perspective on a vertical, essentially real and unconditioned phenomenon. It is seeing the astral from a material point of view. It is reductionism gone awry.

Gods exist, angels exist, and Nirvana exists. Your research must delve into the realms of revelation and intuition. In fighting the astral war, you must match the platform and meet astral onslaughts with astral weapons. To merely reduce everything unfamiliar into social conditions is the attitude of "ignoring it and hoping that it will go away."

Those ignoring the hierarchy of realities will not survive in times ahead. They are destined to be excluded and to exist in a "parallel world simulation, there to live out the remains of their dualistic mindset."

The astral warrior acknowledges his soul, his divine light within. He believes in the hierarchy of realities, the existence of gods, angels, and demigods, and our divine origin, discernible on Earth through history.

These are the astral war realities. This is the battle that is raging.

19. THE RETURN

Regarding the previously mentioned "involution-evolution" dichotomy, in spiritual matters, *involution* precedes *evolution*. Therefore, in this everyday reality of souls living in material bodies, we have to pay proper attention to the fall into materiality, to the involution, the entropy, and the road away from home, before being able to talk about elevation, evolution, negentropy, and the road back home.

One author who highlights the involution-evolution phenomenon is Miguel Serrano. In his essay *NOS – Book of the Resurrection*, we read: "An involution exists, a Golden Age was lost." [p. 78] The sinking of Hyperborea meant the end of the Golden Age, followed by the Silver Age and Iron Age, successively more material and less spiritual eras. It is *the involution of Kali Yuga*. It is the Fall, the road away. This might be seen as a somewhat narrow perspective, while a broader perspective is that the involution began already in heaven, before the dawn of time, before anything material existed, when the Demiurge by rebellion created the material world and let the eternal *eidoi* take tangible form. The involution-evolution concept might allow for some ambiguity in this manner.

Serrano interprets the concept in a mythopoetic way. For instance, later in *NOS,* we have this overview of the mythical meaning of involution:

> In the universe, there is only one history, one civilization, one war, that of the White Gods. All the rest is merely the involution of their Golden Age. You and I are involutions of the White Gods. Quetzalcoatl and Kon-Ticsi Huirakocha were White Gods, like Wotan, Orpheus, Apollo, Siva, Abraxas, Thor and Lucifer. The others, the men of diminished stature who now inhabit the martyrised surface of the Earth, are the surviving slaves of Atlantis and Lemuria, the men-"robots," the men-ants, the animal-men who caused the cataclysm and who will bring about its repetition through their rebelliousness and their ignorant pride. They are the Elementarwesen against whom the Wildes Heer, the Wild Hordes of the Heroes of Parsifal, Odin and Quetzalcoatl will fight their final battle. [p. 130]

In Serrano's *The Golden Cord,* he provides the following perspectives of involution, repeating some of the above along with giving new suggestions:

> We must understand that this world is currently not in evolution but in involution, a spiral downwards. Therefore our reincarnations are degenerating into beasts, animals, etc. Man did not come from the

monkey but rather the monkey comes from the man as a degenerative progression. Battles are being fought everyday between what we call men, animals, dogs, spiders, birds, plants, even between metals. Many do not win the battles and fall by the wayside. Each and every fallen creature has inert energy. This energy is what will give the hero, the Superman, his victory. [Serrano 1978, p 41]

Therefore, involution is *the road away,* the exile, the forgetting, the maze, the labyrinth, entropy, and materialism. However, it is also an experience needed to evolve spiritually—a challenge.

Then, having reached the end of the laborious road, the end of the world – there is a well. Once you have drunk from that well, the well of remembrance (*Mnemosyne*), you remember your first home, the Heimat, Hyperborea. This "un-forgetting" was called "anamnesis" by Plato. After this, you return led by glorified guides, acknowledging your Spiritual Father in God and your spiritual enemy, the Demiurge.

This is the true evolution, spiritual evolution. This is negentropy, the road home, the return, the remembrance, the resurrection. This is the Astral War quest: finding that virtual road back to Hyperborea, opposing anyone trying to stop you from taking it – and telling your brethren of your find, fighting alongside them to regain that Paradise Lost. It is the Prodigal Son, Parsifal, Arthur sailing to Avalon, Siegfried meeting Brünhilde, Orpheus heading for the light, and Odysseus heading for Ithaka. It is Od-Svipdag reuniting with Freya in Agartha-Asgard.

Serrano says that any true astral warrior yearns for something. He is nostalgic; he senses a lost legacy, a lost fatherland. In the miasma of materialism – involution fulfilled – intuition receives a call from out of nowhere, a silent shout calling it back to where it once belonged. It is the spirit yearning for God, the hero for the Valkyrie, the unsung "non-existent path," the mythopoetic path, the artistic-cum-warlike path, and the "spirit of song being war" path.

It is the individual mirroring the whole universal development, the pattern of involution-evolution, entropy-negentropy, from lead to gold, symbolized by the individual's will, vision, thought, and passion. Like Parsifal, he fights his way, inspired by the vision of his female dual, the Hyperborean Valkyrie, his anima.

It is the eternal return, the eternal struggle, the defeat of the Demiurge's materialism, and the acknowledgment of reality's spiritual nature. It is also the victory of the hierarchy of realities, with the soul and Self being more important than the physical body, the astral world being more real than the material world, and Nirvana being more real than the astral.

To endure this war, you must acknowledge will, thought, and passion and embrace Light – to fight desire, darkness, materialism, the Demiurge, and his minions. To fight this war, you must acknowledge your divine origin.

Involution is the Road of Departure. Evolution is the Road of Return. Acknowledge this nature of reality, taught by many wise men, and move intuitively through the maze, guided by the north star, the star leading sailors home, heading for Hyperborea and beyond, the inner Earth of supposed invigorating qualities.

Leave the maze of materialism, the swamp of indulgence, sum up your will, and become a spiritual hero, a vīra, a Sonnenmensch, a sun-man. Become a spiritual superman, fighting his lonely battle against decadence and degeneracy even though he may have no allies nor a female companion – fighting his way, singing his way through nothingness, morally lifting himself by his bootstraps.

It is an astral war, a psychic war, essentially fought in heaven, but the results will be on Earth, as someone said. Those who don't see that will not persevere. To merely reduce the power struggle to tangibility leads out into nothingness, power positivism, and sterility. In essence, it is a mindful war, a conceptual war, a war of nerves. A frequency war.

The subject of "astral war" is indeed stupendous in its scope. It is being fought every second by constant meditation, constant will-guided thinking – by a creative Self in a perpetually existing "now." It is a total war fought by total man, absolute man, Responsible Man. So, if you have what it takes, sum up your will, fuse it with thought, bring passion along, and take the non-existent path, the road back – to Hyperborea and beyond, to Inner Earth and Agartha – fighting your way against the minions of materialism, finally to reach Asgard where the Valkyrie awaits, and you will live in wonder and glory forever.

LITERATURE

Blake, William (in the series *The Penguin Poets*). Introduced and edited by J. Bronowski. Harmondsworth, UK: Penguin Books, 1970

Bulwer–Lytton, Edward. *Vril, the Power of the Coming Race*. First Rate Publishers, sine loco et anno

Doreal, Michael (translator). *The Emerald Tablets of Thoth the Atlantean*. Gallatin, Tennessee: Source Books, 2006

Finlayson Taylor, Christina. *We've Seen the Same Horizon*. West Union, WV: Red Salon, 2019

French, B. J. *The Theosophical Masters: An Investigation into the Conceptual Domains of H. P. Blavatsky and C. W. Leadbeater.* Sydney: University of Sydney, 2000

Jünger, Ernst. Copse 125 (*Das Wäldchen 125, 1925*). London: Chatto & Windus, 1930

Jünger, Ernst. *Heliopolis: Rückblick auf eine Stadt.* Tübingen: Heliopolis Verlag, 1949

Malmberg, Bertil. *Vem spelade mig? A Swedish selection of poems*, introduced and edited by Bengt Holmqvist. Höganäs: Bra Lyrik, 1989

McTaggart, Lynne. *The Field – The Quest for the Secret Force of the Universe.* New York: Harper Perennial, 2008

Melchizedek, Drunvalo. The Ancient Secret of the Flower of Life. Vol 1. *Sine loco*, 1998

Nietzsche, Friedrich. *The Will to Power* (translated by Walter Kaufmann and R. J. Hollingdale). New York:

Random House, 1967

Rydberg, Viktor. *Our Father's Godsaga*. New York: iUniverse, 2003

Schuré, Edouard. *The Great Initiates*. London: William Rider & Sons, 1920

Serrano, Miguel. *NOS – Book of the Resurrection*. London: Routledge & Kegan Paul, 1984

Serrano, Miguel. *The Ultimate Avatar*. Australia: Hermitage Helm Corpus, 2014 (orig. 1984)

Serrano, Miguel. *The Golden Cord*. PDF document (El cordòn dorado, 1978). Translated by Jason Alfred Thompkins. *Sine loco,* 2010

Spengler, Oswald. *The Decline of the West*. First English edition 1926; German original 1918–1922

Svensson, Lennart. *Borderline – A Traditionalist Outlook for Modern Man*. Melbourne: Numen Books, 2015

Svensson, Lennart. *Actionism – How to Become a Responsible Man*. Melbourne: Manticore Books, 2017

Svensson, Lennart. *Ett rike utan like*. Helsingborg: Logik förlag, 2017

Svensson, Lennart. *Science Fiction Seen from the Right*. Melbourne: Manticore Books, 2016

Södergran, Edith. *Samlade dikter*. Stockholm: Wahlström & Widstrand, 1996

Tesla, Nikola. *Mina uppfinningar*. Stockholm: Atlantis, 2000

Tice, Paul. *Vril or Vital Magnetism*. Chicago: McClurg & Co., 1911

van Vogt, A. E. *The World of Null-A*. New York: Berkley Medallion Books, 1970

Wilcock, David. *The Source Field Investigations*. New York: Dutton, 2011

INDEX

ABOUT THE AUTHOR

Lennart Svensson (1965–) is a Sweden–based author. He has, for example, written the books *Actionism – How to Become a Responsible Man, Borderline – A Traditionalist Outlook for Modern Man, Science Fiction Seen from the Right,* and *Ernst Jünger – A Portrait.*